THE
Kitchen Herb
GARDEN

Growing and Preparing Essential Herbs

ROSALIND CREASY

TUTTLE Publishing

Tokyo | Rutland, Vermont | Singapore

Contents

Preface

Growing up, I was an "herb illiterate." All I knew was that, in our house, dill was a flavor in pickles, sage was added to turkey stuffing; and parsley was put on the side of a plate and you never ate it. Today, as my grandmother would say, "I grow an elegant sufficiency" of herbs, most of them in containers conveniently on my front patio. I seldom need to buy them, and I can have herbs that aren't available in most food markets. With a symphony of flavors at my fingertips, I just harvest a few sprigs of sage and/or thyme to kick up the flavor of roasted vegetables, or I can snip a few leaves of chives for egg salad, or add cilantro to a spicy wrap on a whim—much of the year they are all but a few feet away.

Years ago I started growing herbs for their culinary uses but as the time went on I realized that they're integral to a healthy lifestyle. I've even been asked by a few doctors around the country to design mini herb gardens outside their offices so their dietitians can instruct patients on healthier ways to eat. Why are health professionals enthusiastic about herbs? First, most of the culinary herbs are very high in antioxidants—those ingredients in food that are thought to boost our immune system, prevent damage from environmental toxins, and mitigate against some of the effects of aging. Most research indicates they are more effective when taken in food than in supplements. Popular herbs like oregano, rosemary, basil, thyme and cumin are antioxidant-rich, and the ubiquitous parsley, probably the most popular and nutritious herb in the world, is not only high in antioxidants; it is also very high in vitamins C and A, folic acid, and iron.

But that's just one aspect of herbs' healthy side. For those of us who try to limit meat in our diet, herbs can add needed flavor to our meals. I like to substitute herbs for the pepperoni on a pizza. I add a few anise seeds to the sauce and place chopped parsley and oregano under the cheese. Just before serving I sprinkle on a generous amount of fresh chopped basil. In a similar vein, herbs are perfect for folks cutting down on salt.

We've all been exposed to the benefits of herbal teas—chamomile for sleep, peppermint for digestive health, and so on, but instead of buying flavored waters in chemical-laden plastic bottles, why not flavor your home-filtered drinking water with a little lemon balm, cinnamon basil or mint? And instead of air fresheners with their man-made chemical scents, try a small potpourri of sweet smelling anise hyssop and lavender in the living room or a fresh bouquet of Red Ruben basil in the bathroom.

A small patch of fresh herbs can definitely up your game when you entertain. With your herb garden you can create authentic ethnic recipes using herbs you can't find in stores, through simple additions such as sweet woodruff to a traditional German May Wine, Thai basil and lemon grass to your curry, and the delicate chervil to a classic French mesclun salad. Or try some creative ideas I learned when working with chefs, like using the sturdy stems of tall rosemaries as flavorful skewers for kebabs, frying fresh sage leaves for a crunchy topping for a squash, or floating a blue borage flower atop a glass of sparkling water or white wine. (And speaking of borage, for a parlor trick, put a few borage blossoms in a small bowl of white wine vinegar and in about twenty minutes, viola, they turn pink!)

Another advantage of herbs is that they can be a lovely addition to your landscape. Imagine the silvery foliage and fragrant flowers of lavender and the large yellow sprays of fennel flowers as stars in your ornamental border. Picture a green fragrant carpet of sweet woodruff along your shady woodland path, or even a clipped rosemary topiary next to your front porch. Further, in the correct climate and given the right exposure, since they are such healthy growers they usually look their best all season long. Most herbs have few pests and, with good drainage, few diseases. As a bonus, most are drought tolerant. The perennials such as sage, thyme, fennel and oregano only require cutting back in spring (as a bonus, use the trimmings in the coals when you are grilling). In fact, I recommend herbs to my novice landscaping clients, as I consider them edible plants with training wheels.

I'd like to end my homage by pointing out that herbs are a big plus for the environment. Their small flowers, which are preferred by most beneficial insects, including our threatened bees, provide a long season of pollen. Plus those most super of herbs, parsley, and its relatives dill and fennel, also provide food for the black swallowtail larvae. Clearly I can't praise herbs enough!

A Home Herb Garden

What a luxury it is to have a garden full of herbs! Even this country's best chefs usually can't match the meals created from such a garden. Imagine having enough lemon thyme or fennel to be able to use the prunings for smoking pheasant or salmon. Think of creating a salad, as if from the heart of France, with fresh tarragon and chervil, or making a Thai salad with real Thai basil. Fresh herbs are the signature of a chef and often a specific cuisine, yet very few markets in this country offer more than a meager selection.

When I think back on my cooking of years ago, it feels as though I was working in black and white and monaural. The form was there and it was enjoyable, but the depth and richness were missing. Now that I regularly use fresh herbs, I'm cooking in full color and stereo. The zip of fresh mint or the many flavors of thyme give the dishes more dimension. Decades ago I started on my herb adventure by adding fresh chives to potato soup and fresh basil to spaghetti sauce. What a difference! I went on to use fresh dill on fish, pesto on pasta, and herb vinegars on salads. Now, after years of exposure to the full range of herbs, and thanks to many people's guidance, I use many more in my cooking, and most of the year they are fresh.

There are dozens of varieties of thyme and I chose six different ones to set off my bird bath (**LEFT**). In the perimeter beds I planted chives, scented geraniums, golden sage, and a selection of salad greens. To unify this little garden I included the showy, but poisonous, tall graceful foxgloves and blue star creeper (*Laurentia fluviatilis*) in between the boards.

This harvest of fresh herbs (LEFT) is every chef's dream. Included are many of the stars of the culinary herb garden; (CLOCKWISE FROM THE TOP) chives, French thyme, purple sage, sage flowers, silver lemon thyme, sage buds, rosemary, and French tarragon. In the middle are sprigs of Italian flat-leaf parsley and the flowers of German chamomile.

RIGHT: A small collection of herb containers adorns my rose patio. The pineapple mint, sage, and lemon balm shown here grow well in all but the hottest humid climates.

Herbs are the easiest to grow of all the edible plants and are great for beginning gardeners. Another incentive is that cooking with herbs can be a very healthful way to add excitement to meals. At a time when the safety of the salt and fats in our diet is being seriously questioned, it's a relief to explore enjoyable substitutes. I get so tired of being deprived in the effort to be "good." Using herbs deepens the pleasure as well as the healthfulness of food.

As I mentioned, my education in herb cookery started slowly. I was always an avid gardener, so years ago I put in a basil plant or two and some dill and chives, and that's still a good way to start. My serious interest in herbs took hold when I visited the herb garden at Caprilands in Coventry, Connecticut. This extensive garden, fueled by the enthusiasm of the late Adelma Simmons, actually contained many different kinds of herb gardens: one that attracts butterflies, an all-gray one, a garden full of scented geraniums, and another with herbs for drying. At Caprilands, my sister and I enjoyed a meal in which herbs were used in each course, and Adelma came around while we ate to talk about which ones we were enjoying. That trip to Caprilands opened my eyes to the vast world of herbs and their many possibilities.

Since then I have visited many public herb gardens, and I highly recommend them to other interested gardeners and cooks. Visiting these gardens is a great way to learn to identify the appearance, smell, and flavor of individual herbs. This country has hundreds of beautiful public herb gardens. Try a visit to our nation's herb garden in Washington, D.C., at the United States National Arboretum, or to the Cloisters, with its wonderful medieval garden, in New York City. Or sample herbs at the magnificent formal herb gardens at the Missouri and Chicago botanical gardens and the historical gardens at Old Sturbridge Village and Monticello. All grow a wonderful range of herbs and usually provide a guide to help you identify them.

Once I had a working knowledge of most of the herbs, I found I needed the help of creative cooks to explore herbs in the kitchen. For every one way I thought of to use an herb, someone like herb maven Carole Saville or Rose Marie Nichols McGee (who was raised in the shadow of Nichols Garden Nursery, a well-known herb supplier) had created ten. And in the hands of master chefs such as the late Tom McCombie of Chez T.J.'s in Mountain View, California, and Ron Zimmerman of the Herbfarm outside Seattle, Washington, dishes came alive with herbs.

Both Carole Saville and Rose Marie McGee grew demonstration gardens for this book to put their creative information together and show us how simply and elegantly herb gardens can be created. In the process, they shared much information on how to maintain and cook from these gardens.

One final comment before we proceed. You might be totally unacquainted with some of the herbs covered here. In my research I was struck by how much of our available information and our emphasis on growing and cooking herbs comes from Europe. This is a wonderful bank of knowledge, but it excludes the many cultures around the world that season their foods with native plants. These so-called exotic herbs have a place in the new world cuisine, and I have included them here. I know you will find them as exciting as I have.

Golden sage, chives, French thyme, Spanish lavender, and rosemary in containers (LEFT) greet visitors to my garden. In the beds curly parsley, winter savory, Chinese chives, oregano, and flowers line the walk.

How to Plant a Herb Garden

The late Jim Wilson, who owned Savory Farms wholesale herb growers, came to visit me one day, and as he walked up my herb-lined front path, he became completely engrossed in the plants before I could usher him into the house. He kept leaning down and rubbing his hands over the foliage. "Your thyme and tarragon grow so much more lushly than ours," he said. "We have problems with nematodes and wilt diseases." He was clearly envious of the 'Greek' oregano.

Jim, probably best known to most gardeners as the one-time Southern host of the *Victory Garden* television show, grew his herbs in humid South Carolina in a climate very different from that of dry California. As we renewed our old friendship, the subject of herbs came up again and again, and we compared notes about the different species and how they grew in the different parts of the country. How, say, lovage and angelica might grow to seven feet tall in New York, yet only to three feet tall in Texas; how scented geraniums are perennial and five feet tall across in San Diego but grow as annuals only two feet tall in Idaho. Despite the differences, though, we were struck by how most gardeners can grow most herbs and how all can have a wonderful time doing it.

Growing Herbs

The majority of herbs are perennial plants that need six to eight hours of sun daily, very well drained soil, little fertilizing, and spring pruning for renewal. In areas of the country where the ground freezes, most might need only mulch-

LEFT: A harvest of unusual culinary herbs includes a red monarda flower, lavender, scented geraniums, golden oregano, and rose hips.
BELOW: There's virtually no end to the number of herbs that can grow happily in containers.

ing, although tender herbs such as rosemary and lemon verbena must be brought inside in the winter in cold climates. Alternatively, they can be treated as annuals and replanted every spring. In arid climates they need irrigation (drip irrigation is ideal) and should be washed down occasionally to prevent spider mites.

In hot, humid climates, where plants are bothered by nematodes, fungus diseases, and high heat, perennial herbs can be planted every year in a new area of the garden or in containers. Gwen Barclay and her mother, the late Madalene Hill, the Texas-based authors of *Southern Herb Growing*, had much success avoiding many diseases and mitigating the extreme heat by growing their herbs in raised beds and by mulching the plants with small-diameter gravel, sometimes called chicken scratch. The gravel helps promote drainage and reflects summer heat, thereby keeping the soil fairly cool.

The annual herbs, such as basil, dill, chervil, and cilantro, are grown in a somewhat different manner, as they need annual planting and better soil than the perennials.

In most cases, there are solutions to most cultural problems that might arise with herbs, and even gardeners with no yard at all can grow a few herbs on a sunny windowsill.

Herb plants can be planted in a simple dooryard cluster, in a flower border, in containers, or in a traditional formal knot garden, so-called because the plants are laid out to form intricate patterns when viewed from above. As a rule, because they need similar growing conditions, annual herbs are at home in a bed of annual flowers and/or vegetables or clustered together. Perennial herbs grow best surrounded by other perennial flowers and herbs. For ease of maintenance, the informal cluster of perennial herbs is hard to beat. But, if a formal knot garden has always been your dream, be prepared to give continual care. The plants will need constant clipping to look their best. Whatever your choice regarding garden design, the most important factor concerning your herb garden is how close it is to the house. All the

The herbs—nepitella (**BOTTOM LEFT CORNER**) and chives (**CENTER**)—grow in a border of edible flowers including nasturtiums, violas, calendulas, and arugula. All thrive in full sun and moist, organic soil.

herb authorities I agree that the closer your herbs are to the kitchen door, the more you will use them in your cooking.

The following section describes a small herb garden and covers general herb-growing basics, from planting to maintenance, based on the experiences of Rose Marie Nichols McGee and Carole Saville. Their gardens are more complex and show how varied herb gardens can be. Many gardeners are interested in container herbs, so that information is covered in the next section. The nitty-gritty of growing herbs is covered in Appendixes A and B. Appendix A has information on planning an herb garden, bed preparation, mulching, planting, irrigation methods, fertilizing, and composting. Appendix B provides an overall look at beneficial insects and the basics of pest and disease control. Let's start with a prototype starter herb garden.

Herb Garden Basics

Before you begin growing many herbs, it helps to know that the great majority of them fall into two major categories: perennials, herbs that live for more than two seasons, and annuals, those herbs that live only one season. When you begin, it also helps to choose herbs that are generally easy to grow. In most climates these are the sun-loving perennials: thyme, oregano, French tarragon, and chives. All originated in Europe and, with the exception of chives, are drought-tolerant and need little fertilizing unless grown in sandy soils. In hot, humid climates and mild desert regions French tarragon can't tolerate the heat, so you might want to try Mexican tarragon (*Tagetes lucida*) instead, which is also easily grown and may be available from local nurseries (or ordered from many of the sources listed in the back of the book). The popular perennial herbs can be purchased as small plants at most local nurseries from spring through early fall.

There are few gardeners who grow herbs and don't include basil. While still easily grown, basil needs annual planting every spring, rich soil, and some TLC.

Basil and cilantro seeds are available from your local nursery, but most beginning gardeners find it easiest to grow them from young nursery transplants. (If you prefer to start your own seeds, see "Starting from Seeds" in Appendix A.) When selecting your plants, avoid those that look yellow or wilted or have started to flower. (Note: In some nurseries seedlings are sold six plants or so to a small 4-inch (about 10 cm) container. When you take it home, gently separate the young plants and plant them out. Failure to separate the plants will create a sorry clump.) By the way, hold off planting your cilantro until late summer, as it quickly goes to flower in the spring.

For your first herb garden, I suggest planting one plant each of thyme, tarragon, and oregano, two chive plants, and three or four basil plants. If you're new to cooking with herbs, learning to grow and becoming comfortable cooking with these tried-and-true herbs will be all you need to make a dramatic change in your cooking as well as your gardening.

Planting Your Herb Garden

Gardeners in cold-winter areas will do best to plant in the spring or early summer; gardeners in mild climates will be able to plant all but basil and cilantro through the fall. To plant your herbs, clear an area of the garden that gets at least six hours (eight is better) of midday sun and has great drainage. If you live in a cool-summer area, try to locate the garden near masonry to give extra heat for the basil. In hot-summer areas herbs grow best with late-afternoon shade. An area 4 x 6 feet (1.2 x 1.8 m) will be enough for the suggested herbs.

Remove rocks and any clods, rake the area smooth, and spread 4–5 inches (10–12 cm) of organic matter or compost over the soil. With a spading fork, work it into the top 6 inches (15 cm).

Place your herbs with the short ones—thyme and chives—in the front, tarragon in the middle, and the taller oregano and basil in the back. Thyme and chives will spread to about a foot (30 cm), the others up to 2 feet (0.6 m), so space them accordingly. Dig a hole about a foot (30 cm) across for each herb and sprinkle a few tablespoons of bonemeal or other form of phosphorus around the bottom of each hole and mix it in well. In the holes for the basil plants, add a few coffee cans full of manure or good compost, then add a source of nitrogen such as a few tablespoons of blood meal or fish meal. Mix the amendments into the bottom of the hole.

My front entry overflows with herbs. In the ground are the showy society garlic (the mauve flowers are used in salads), chives, savory, borage, and thyme. In containers are nutmeg geranium, and many different sages and thymes.

To prepare the soil (**TOP LEFT**), spread 4 inches (10 cm) of compost and 2 inches (5 cm) of manure over the soil and work it in with a spading fork. Dig a hole four times the size of the herb's root ball and work in ¼ cup each of blood meal and bonemeal. Plant the herb at the depth it was in the container (**TOP RIGHT**) and press down around the plant. Install drip irrigation and mulch (**ABOVE**) with 2 inches (5 cm) of compost.

Gently nudge each herb seedling out of its container by putting your hand over the top of the container, turning it over, and tapping it to loosen the plant. If roots are collected in a mass around the outside of the root ball, gently pull them apart and spread them out. Put the plant in its hole, making sure the crown of the plant is level with the bed. Cover the seedling with soil and firm it in place so there will be no air pockets.

If you are putting in a drip watering system, this is the time to lay your ooze tubing around the plants and secure them. Make a small watering basin around the plant and fill it with water. (Many gardeners find it helpful to put a label next to each type of plant so they can identify their herbs.) Water a final and critical time to make sure all the roots have received a soaking. Mulch the area with 2–3 inches (5–8 cm) of mulching material to cut down on weeding and watering. Watch for slugs and earwigs on the basil—a flashlight foray the night after a watering will usually

tions on the package. If you don't have a chance to harvest your basil, when it gets large and starts to flower you will need to prune it back by taking clippers and removing the top half of the shoots. This will encourage the plant to put out lush new leaves instead of setting seeds and declining. Unless the soil is sandy, the rest of the herbs seldom need fertilizer.

Prune all the perennial herbs using hedge or hand shears in late spring. Most herbs need to be cut back by at least half, though if the plants are not growing vigorously, remove only a third of the growth. Oregano and thyme are only hardy to USDA Zone 5, or to -10 to -20°F (-12.2 to -29°C); chives to USDA Zone 3, or to -50 to -40°F (-45.5 to -40°C); tarragon to USDA Zone 4, or -30 to -20°F (-34.4 to -20°C); and in cold climates, all will overwinter best with 3–4 inches (8–10 cm) of a straw or compost mulch layered over them in the fall after the ground has frozen. The mulch is not used to keep them warm but to ensure that they will not heave out of the ground when the soil freezes and thaws.

reveal these critters. Pick them by hand and drop them in soapy water to kill them.

Keep the new plants moist for the first week or so. Slowly start letting the plants get a little drier between waterings. Use your judgment—if it's very hot or windy, or if the plants start to wilt, water more often. If weeds come through the mulch, pull them so they will not compete with the herbs for water and nutrients.

Maintaining Your Herb Garden

After a few months your herbs will be growing well, and a watering maintenance schedule will become established. In climates where rain is reliable, you will probably need to water only during a drought or in very hot weather. In arid climates a weekly routine is sufficient for all but basil and cilantro, which may need watering every four or five days.

Fertilize basil every six weeks or so with fish emulsion or fish meal according to the direc-

TOP: After a few months the basil is in full production and the chives, tarragon, and thyme are ready for harvest.
ABOVE: Most common herbs and a few unusual ones are available from local nurseries in small plastic containers. It's important to label your plants so you can identify them, especially those that are less common. In addition, I find I need to record the location and planting date of my new herbs in a journal because the labels sometimes get lost or become faded.

Harvesting Your Herbs

For me, harvesting herbs often means a last-minute dash to the garden to pick a few leaves for cooking. When I have it together, though, I harvest a number of my favorite herbs and put them in a glass of water and place them on the windowsill above my sink. I then use them with abandon—all I need do is reach for a sprig or two. If I want to keep the herbs longer, I put them (all but basil) in the refrigerator, and they'll keep fresh for at least a week.

To harvest larger amounts for preserving, choose a time when the herbs are at peak flavor, usually just before flowering, and when the plants are growing well enough to renew themselves. Another good time to harvest is when the plants need to be cut back to be renewed. Then one of the luxuries of having an herb garden is most evident, as you can use large amounts of the prunings for smoking. When you smoke fish or meat, place branches of green herbs such as thyme, lavender, fennel, rosemary, or dill over the wet wood chips before you close up the smoker. Voilà, lots of instant flavor.

Harvesting the Seeds of Herbs

To harvest the seeds from dill, caraway, cumin, coriander, and fennel, start to assess their ripeness a few weeks after the plants bloom and when the seed heads start to turn brown. The seed heads of dill and fennel will shatter and shed their seeds more readily than the other herbs, and if you want

This basket (LEFT) overflows with a harvest from my front herb border. It includes the unusual dittany of Crete (*Origanum dictamnus*), which is used in liqueurs, spilling out of the front, Mexican tarragon (*Tagetes lucida*), which is sometimes used in place of French tarragon, the mauve edible flowers of society garlic (*Tulbaghia violacea*), and bunches of rosemary, (BACK LEFT), and oregano (BACK RIGHT).

to make sure to harvest all the seeds, tie a paper bag around the ripening seed head to catch the seeds. In all cases you can remove the seeds by hand once they have turned brown, or you can harvest the whole heads, leaving 6 inches (15 cm) of stem attached so you can tie the stems together. Dry the heads by hanging them upside down. First put a brown bag around the heads, secure it with a rubber band, and hang the bunches in a cool, dry place. When the heads are thoroughly dry, pull the seeds off the heads, put them in clean jars, and seal.

Preserving Herbs

Fresh herbs are best in many cases, but most herbs are not available year-round, so good cooks over the years have learned ways to preserve the flavor. The best way to preserve an herb depends on the herb. As a rule, the dense, small-leafed herbs dry best, and the fleshy, larger leaves freeze well, either chopped or in butters. Most herbs are suitable for preserving in vinegar or oil.

Drying Herbs

The following directions for drying herbs are best used for bay laurel, borage, chamomile, marjoram, mint, rosemary, sage, bay, chives, dill, lavender, lemon verbena, Mexican oregano, sweet woodruff, thyme, winter savory, and oregano.

Harvest all herbs in the driest part of the day and wash them if they're gritty, and pat them dry. There are different ways to pick and dry them. Some methods work best for herbs with large leaves, others for those with small leaves. You can easily pick the single large leaves of sweet bay, lemon verbena, and borage and lay them out in a single layer on a screen; the long leaves of chives can be treated this way as well. I find it tedious to harvest herbs with small leaves and compact stems, such as thyme, rosemary, savory, chamomile, and sweet woodruff, as single leaves. I prune sprigs three or 4 inches (10 cm) long and lay them out on a screen; once the herbs are dry, the leaves can easily be stripped off the twigs. In all cases, for quick drying, you can put the screen with the leaves on it in an oven at a very low temperature (105°F/40°C) for a few hours.

If you have more time, place the screen in a warm, dry place indoors, such as a garage or attic, and dry for five to seven days. Stir the leaves once a day.

Herbs that grow fairly tall and produce long sprays, such as oregano, sage, mint, lavender, and lemon verbena, can be dried by hanging them in a warm, dry place. Create bunches bundled with a rubber band to hold the sprays together. (The rubber band will also hold them when they dry and shrink.) As I do this in my dusty garage, I like to cover the bundles with tissue paper to keep the herbs clean. Seed heads of dill, fennel, and caraway I handle in the same way, but I also put a paper bag over the heads so the seeds will not drop to the floor.

Some gardeners swear by drying herbs in the microwave oven. This works well for a small amount, but I do find that the leaves get darker than when air-dried. Place cleaned herbs on a piece of paper towel and microwave them on high for a minute at a time. Rotate the herbs often. Repeat the process until the herbs are brittle dry. Dense herbs like rosemary will take longer than delicate ones like dill. When your herbs are dry, store them in airtight containers in a cool, dark place.

Freezing Herbs

You can also preserve some herbs by freezing. I do this with fennel, dill, chervil, chives, tarragon, and mint. Just wash the herbs, pat them dry, and take the leaves off the stems. Leave them whole or chop them. Put the leaves in a self-sealing plastic freezer bag, press out the air, label, and freeze. You do not need to defrost them before using them in soups, sauces, and marinades. The herbs will have darkened and turned soft, but the flavor keeps for a good six months. Herbal butters are another way to freeze the flavor of herbs. (See the recipe on page 79.)

Garden sages (**LEFT**) can spark the cook's imagination, all the way from deep-frying until crisp and used as a garnish to making fritters with the flowering stalks, or adding the leaves when you roast potatoes, and using the unusual foliage for garnishes.

Designing Your Herb Garden

As a landscape designer, I feel compelled to share with you a few of my own personal herb gardens and the design process I went through.

My favorite herb garden is the one I had installed in the front yard many years ago. Instead of using the plants as the major feature, I used a strong geometric pattern formed by putting 2 × 12-inch (5 x 30 cm) boards in the ground in a ray pattern. For the focal point in the middle I placed a birdbath.

I got the wood for free from the lumberyard since they had been cut off the end of larger boards that had been milled for other projects. (It took six months of visiting lumberyards, but it was worth it.) The boards were cut into long wedges and scored on the back with ⅛-inch (3-mm)-deep grooves to prevent them from cupping. They were then laid out in a ray pattern and secured in place by two layers of bender board nailed to both sides of the circle. I used all sorts of culinary herbs around the outside and toward the middle: thymes, oreganos, lavenders, tarragon, lemon balm, and chives, along with a few salad greens and disease-resistant roses. Within a year the ground cover had filled in and the plants looked mature enough to make it a magical garden. We still refer to it as the Magic Circle (see pages 30-31).

Another herb planting I enjoy is the herbal entry up my front steps and walk. In this case, while the steps and walk add design interest, it's the herbs and flowering plants that get the attention. I chose purple, yellow, and light pink as the color theme and filled in other parts of the garden with lots of variegated herbs. I think their white-and-green and white-and-gold leaves make a perfect foil for the deep hues of yellow and purple. I chose variegated lemon thyme, golden and tricolor sage, and golden oregano as the stars of the front border and added yellow violas in the spring and yellow species marigolds in the summer.

The McGee Herb Garden

Rose Marie Nichols McGee grew up in Oregon next door to an herb nursery. Maybe I can be forgiven, therefore, when I say that she knows herbs from the ground up. For years I ordered herbs from her parents' company, Nichols Garden Nursery (www.nicholsgardennursery.com), which continues to be family-owned. It seemed natural to contact the McGees when I was searching for knowledgeable people to share information on herbs.

Rose Marie was very enthusiastic about growing a demonstration garden for me. She saw it as a great excuse to put in a small herb garden for her late mother. Her mother had been hampered by arthritis for some years and missed having a garden. What a wonderful little garden the new one turned out to be! Rose Marie cut a modified kidney-shaped area, about 10 x 20 feet (3 x 6 m) in size, out of an existing lawn and filled it completely with herbs. The idea, she told me, was to make "an informal and inviting little oasis, with paths so my mother—or anyone!—could get right in and enjoy it."

The bed preparation was rather straightforward. Rose Marie began in late spring by digging up the area and then, to save a lot of weeding in the future, sifted through the soil to remove all the rhizomes of the weedy quack grass that had grown rampantly in the lawn. She then put on a layer of mushroom compost and hand tilled it in. Finally, to prevent another future problem and to give the garden a clean line, Rose Marie put in a black plastic edging to keep the lawn from growing into the herb bed.

One design objective was low maintenance, which meant making a perennial garden with spaces reserved for annual herbs like basil, calendulas, cilantro, dill, and nasturtiums. She explained: "This year, because it's new, I've added many annuals, but by next year the perennials will fill it in and be in their glory and I won't add many annuals. I enjoy having a constant supply of flowers and color in the garden for most of the season, so I chose many of the flowers to bloom at different times of the year."

Rose Marie decided to start the blooming season with sweet cicely, which blossoms in spring along with the daffodils and has white, lacy, very fragrant flowers. Other herbs that will bloom throughout the growing season include clary sage, which produces great spikes of lavender flowers; regular chives, with their lavender blossoms pro-

Pink, purple, and yellow flowers give warmth to my herb entry and help tie together the great variety of plants. The walk is lined with yellow species marigolds and gloriosa daisies, purple sage, and pink roses. The herbs include curly parsley, oregano, tricolor and golden sages, winter savory, anise hyssop, society garlic, and dittany of Crete.

duced in late spring; Chinese chives, with white flowers that smell like roses and that bloom in July and August; two varieties of lavender that bloom most of the summer; lemon mint, which will provide a lot of color in late August with its shaggy purple heads; and pineapple sage for late-fall color—its scarlet blossoms will brighten up the garden from September until it is cut down by frost and dies. During the first year annual plants yielded much of the garden's color—the purple foliage of 'Red Rubin' basil, orange and yellow nasturtiums and calendulas, and the large yellow heads of dill.

The garden was designed with low edging plants in the front and along the paths, with a gradual increase in the height of the plants toward the middle and back. Rose Marie used as focal points for the design a dramatic angelica plant, with its large spreading leaves and handsome foliage, and two graceful statues of monks made by a local artist.

I asked Rose Marie to talk a bit about how she uses herbs from the garden. "I harvest angelica when it's just starting to bloom," she began, "because that's when it has the most flavor. I don't let the flower heads develop at all. I then simply take the large stems and cut them up and boil them in a sugar syrup. Once they're candied and dried, I chop the stems and add them to my favorite shortbread recipe. Another herb I enjoy is sweet cicely. I use the foliage in salads during the year and the seeds in fruit or green salads. The seeds are tender and have a sweet anise flavor."

There was a great deal of basil in the garden, and I asked Rose Marie how she prepared it. She told me that she preserves it by chopping the leaves and layering them in a jar alternately with layers of Parmesan cheese and then freezing it. She finds that it keeps very well that way, and she sprinkles basil on vegetables and salads and uses it in pesto and spaghetti sauce all winter long.

On my last day at Rose Marie's garden, she laid out a marvelous tea party—the very vision of a childhood fantasy, complete with scones with scented basil jellies, shortbread with candied angelica, and lemon verbena tea. All the confections were wonderful, and all were filled with herbs!

Designing Your Herb Garden

You can start herb gardening in numerous ways. For example, a few annual plants of basil, dill, chervil, and cilantro can be spotted around your vegetable garden or interplanted among flowers. In this case little soil preparation is needed beyond what you have done for the existing vegetables and flowers. Adding an occasional perennial herb like lavender, Chinese chives, sage, fennel, and thyme to a perennial flower border is easy too. Just loosen the soil and place the transplant in the soil, water it in and mulch the soil, water it again off and on for the first few weeks, and let the rains (or drip irrigation) and Mother Nature take over. If you are a beginning herb gardener and want to plant just a few herbs in a corner of your yard, then you might consult "Herb Garden Basics" on page 14. However, if you are planning a fairly extensive new herb garden, you will need to prepare the soil more carefully and design the beds for ease of access and for appearance.

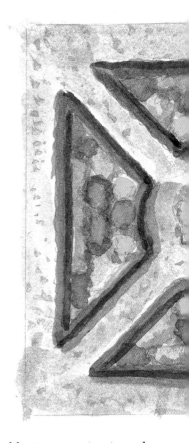

The Nichols garden and the Saville garden (shown on page 81) are examples of two completely different layout styles that would work in any garden. The Nichols garden is an informal cluster of herbs in a free-form design located in the middle of a lawn. It is easy to install, and its informality requires little maintenance, as plants don't need to be continually pruned to be kept to a specific shape and size. The Saville garden, in contrast, is a more formal design and will take a few years for the hedges to become established. While certainly not high-maintenance, it will require more care than the Nichols garden. Consider too my herb gardens—an entry garden with steps up the walk, a circular herb garden built around a birdbath, and a streetside herb border. Look too to the dozens of geometric traditional herb garden designs. Whether you choose an informal area on either side of your front walk, create an informal shape in the lawn, or install a formal herb garden off your patio, plan for an area not much more than 400 square feet (122 m). This is a good size for most gardeners and

gardens. It is a manageable size to maintain and has room for dozens of different herbs. For most designs, first lay out either strings or hoses along the ground to give you an idea of the area and a feel for the size and shape.

Installing a Formal Herb Garden

If you want to install a traditional geometric herb garden, either of the two following simple and straightforward formal designs are an easy way to start. Mark off an area 20 x 20 feet (6 x 6 m). For the first design (see drawing, top left), create bisecting paths that cut across the diagonal in an x and create four equal triangular beds. Another option is to choose bisecting paths that cross each other in the middle and form a cross, creating four squares (see page 27, top right). To make both designs more interesting, place a square or round bed in the middle and put a focal point sundial, sculpture, or birdbath in the middle. Paths through any type of herb garden should be at least 3 feet (1 m) across to give ample room to walk and use a wheelbarrow. Beds are generally

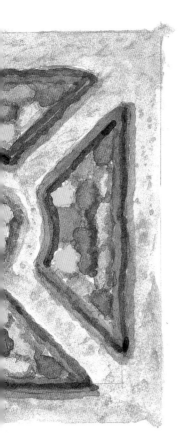

limited to 5 feet (1.5m) across, as that is the average distance a person can reach into the bed to harvest or pull weeds from both sides. Consider putting a fence, wall, or hedge around the herb garden to give it a stronger design, and to keep out critters if need be.

Designers use many different techniques to create the feeling of formality. Here are a few tips for planning your own garden.

• Create formal gardens using geometric shapes—not free-form lines.
• Use small hedges, traditionally boxwood, dwarf English lavender, or germander, to outline the beds and sometimes the perimeter.
• Clipped hedges and herbs or topiaries give a decidedly formal feeling to a garden.
• When you use the same plant many times (especially when you repeat them in the same location in all the geometric beds), it tightens the design and makes a garden feel more formal.
• Line paths of formal gardens with paving, gravel, or lawn grasses, not straw or compost.

ABOVE LEFT: My magic circle herb garden is large, measuring 40 x 40 feet (12 x 12 m), and has room for many herbs and a few salad greens. It is a fairly formal design in that I used large plants to anchor the corners, created a geometric form in the middle, and placed similar colors and shapes of plants in repetitive patterns around the center. If I had wanted it to be more formal I would have used small clipped hedges to circle the birdbath and around the outside. Further, I would have repeated the same herbs in the perimeter beds.

ABOVE MIDDLE Bisecting paths cut across the sides of this formal herb garden. A round bed is cut out of the center and a focal point container is placed in the center. A small hedge borders the beds and yellow flowers are used at each inside corner to add interest. The second design (**ABOVE**) is also geometric. Here a square bed is cut in the middle and given a fancy plant for a focal point. Repetitive plants have been used on the corners and the garden has been fenced to give it a sense of enclosure.

• Formal gardens usually include a focal point or two to interest the eye. Place these in the middle of the garden, on the four corners, or in the middle of each geometric bed. Focal points can be plants in containers, birdbaths, statuary, or very showy plants such as tree roses or herbs with unusual foliage.

This informal Texas herb garden (BELOW) belongs to Lucinda Hutson, author of many herb books. The terracotta statue gives it a regional identity, as does the informal bench in the background. Both act as focal points and unify the design. Rosemary, oregano, society garlic, and arugula that has gone to flower spill out of the beds with abandon.

I designed this hillside herb garden (BOTTOM) with creeping thyme around the paving stones, and yarrows, rosemary, lavenders, and society garlic around the paths. More culinary herbs follow down the hill and include sages, fennel, and chives. The deer on the property have the consideration to leave them all alone.

ABOVE: This lovely formal herb garden is at the Minneapolis Arboretum. Many cities have public herb gardens and they are a rewarding way to see how different herbs perform in your climate. The boxwood hedges, brick walk and edgings, and the geometric shapes of the beds give a sense of formality. Container plants are used as focal points. Here they contain rosemary and sweet bay, two plants that will not winter over in harsh winters, but that can be brought inside to a sun room or greenhouse. The arbors and trellises create outdoor rooms and give a feeling of enclosure to this garden. A similar effect can be used in the home garden to frame an herb garden, but the dimensions of the structures should be smaller and more in keeping with the intimacy of a home garden.

My magic circle herb garden (**ABOVE**) was made with eighteen, slightly tapered, 3-foot-long wooden boards in a circle around a birdbath. I chose blue star creeper for the ground cover to fill in between the boards, and for color, foxgloves with their pink spires. (Be aware the foxgloves are poisonous.) It includes many varieties of thyme, chives, scented geraniums, cilantro, arugula, tarragon, lavenders, and sages.

I designed a small crescent-shaped bed (**TOP RIGHT**) with thyme, Chinese and garden chives, society garlic, and variegated oregano to be the focal point for my vegetable garden. Within six months it had filled in (**RIGHT**) and made a graceful entrance to the garden.

Growing Herbs in Containers

I plant many herbs in my garden, but I've noticed that nowadays I'm growing an increasing number in containers—herbs on the patio are oh-so-handy to the kitchen, and, further, using herbs in containers gives me a range of design options. I liken it to hanging pictures in a room—spotting containers around my garden adds interest. If I feel like bright primary colors, I bring out my enamel containers; if I want a cottage-garden effect, I use my aged terracotta favorites.

Growing herbs in containers is also valuable for gardeners with small yards and for people forced to grow edibles in containers because their soil is infested with nematodes or root rots. In addition, as containers can be brought inside, in harsh-winter areas container growing may be the best way to grow tender perennials like rosemary and sweet marjoram.

How to Grow Herbs in Containers

After years of trial and error, I've found five secrets for success with growing herbs in containers:

1. I use only soil mixes formulated for containers. I've found that garden soil drains poorly and pulls away from the sides of the container, allowing most of the water to run out, and it is often filled with weed seeds.

2. Since containers must have drainage holes in the bottom to prevent the plant from drowning, at planting time I cover the holes with a piece of window screening or small square of weed cloth to keep dirt in and slugs out. (New evidence indicates that gravel or pottery shards in the bottom actually interfere with drainage.)

3. In hot weather, I now use only large containers, those large enough to provide generously for the plant's root system and hold enough soil so that the plant needs to be watered less often. I find that a small number of the small herbs like chives and thyme will grow in 12-inch (30-cm) containers, but most grow best in large containers (18 inches/ 46 cm or more in diameter). My Southern friends report that in their climate large containers are mandatory, as the roots on the south side of small pots bake in the hot sun.

4. After years of pale plants, I find I need to fertilize frequently and evenly. For me, biweekly doses of fish emulsion work well, as do granulated fish meal and slow-release fertilizer granules renewed every six weeks or so.

5. I find the most difficult aspect of container growing is to maintain the correct moisture in the soil. Succulent herbs like basil and chervil suffer when not watered enough; on the other hand, the Mediterranean drought-tolerant herbs succumb to root rot if given too much water, especially the sages. Once I learned how to water properly, I was on the road to success.

All gardeners need to learn to water container plants properly; even in rainy climates, hand-watering containers is usually a necessity, as little rain penetrates the umbrella of foliage covering a pot. I find that when I hand water, it is most helpful to water the container twice. The first time premoistens the soil (I think of it as moistening a dry sponge), and the second watering is when I

Herbs make handsome container plants (**LEFT**). They are compact, have a lovely range of foliage colors and textures, and most bloom at least once a year. Here the foliage of a purple sage contrasts with yellow and orange nasturtium flowers, and the spiky texture of the chives sets off the rounded nasturtium leaves.

feel as though I am actually watering the soil. The opposite of underwatering is overwatering. To prevent this, I test the soil moisture content with my finger before watering.

Watering container-grown herbs is critical for all gardeners, but it's of even greater importance for those of us who live in arid climates. After years of parched-looking plants, I finally installed a drip system. What a difference! I use Antelco's emitters, called "shrubblers" (available from plumbing supply stores and online) as they are tailored so each container on the system can have the exact amount of water it needs. My drip system is connected to an automatic timer, so it's scheduled to water every night for five minutes from spring through fall. I encourage you to go online and check out the many instructional videos available on making use of this type of system.

Overwintering Herbs Indoors

As you can see, growing plants outside in containers has its challenges, and the problems are exacerbated when you bring the plants inside for the winter. In essence, you change a plant's environment from a bright, sunny spot with fairly high humidity and a normal ecosystem and relocate it to a dim area with low humidity and no natural predators. It can be done, and done well, but it requires care, thought, the right plants, and a suitable sunny spot in the house. As a rule, herbs that tolerate shade are the most successful. If you plan to cook with many of the herbs, you will need more plants than usual, as herbs grown indoors over the winter grow more slowly than those outside.

It's late spring in my garden and time to pot up young tarragon, lavender, and scented geraniums before the weather gets too hot and they need water twice a day. A harvest of curly parsley, to make a lovely cream soup, oregano for drying, and the purple flowers of the Mexican sage (*Salvia leucantha*) for a table bouquet, complete the scene.

1. Select a place in the house that gets at least six hours of direct sun a day. Temperatures in the 60–70°F (15–21°C) range and areas away from cold drafts are best. If a sunny window is not available, then set up an area with grow lights. Locate fixtures 6 inches (15 cm) above the plants, and run them for sixteen hours a day.

2. Choose herbs that are fairly adaptable to indoor conditions, such as mint, parsley, winter savory, lemon balm, and scented geraniums. Chives grow fairly well indoors but tend to go dormant for part of the winter. If you have an attached greenhouse or bright sunroom, you might try the sun-loving bay, oregano, rosemary, sweet marjoram, and thyme as well.

3. For the best success, choose your plants at the beginning of the growing season and plant them in containers from the outset instead of uprooting

ABOVE: Containers can become the focal point of a garden. Here an old wooden bucket filled with golden sage and a nail barrel with ornamentals and creeping rosemary draw the eye. In the background the flower spikes of anise hyssop attract bees, and in the foreground a winter savory peeks out from behind a species yellow marigold.

RIGHT: Two large 'Tuscan Blue' rosemary trees and two sages, the purple 'Purpurascens' and a gray-leafed 'Extrakta,' in blue containers, adorn my front steps.

them in the fall. Containers at least 8 inches (20 cm) across filled with commercial potting soil do best. These containers can be sunk in garden soil over the summer to keep watering to a minimum.

4. A few weeks before your first expected frost, prune back plants; check for aphids, scale, whiteflies, and mites; and treat if infested.

5. Place plants in a shady spot for a few weeks to acclimatize them to low light levels.

6. Just before bringing plants in, wash remaining

foliage well and spray with a prophylactic dose of insecticidal soap.

7. Once they're inside, isolate outdoor plants from your houseplants until you have determined that neither is contaminated.

8. Water most overwintering plants only when the soil surface starts to dry out.

9. Wash down foliage occasionally to remove dust that can harbor spider mites.

10. Turn containers every week or so, so all sides receive equal light.

11. Fertilize monthly with half-strength fertilizer.

12. Maintain good air circulation and keep plants from touching, to prevent diseases and pests.

13. If your house is very dry, raise the humidity around your plants by filling a shallow tray with pebbles and placing it under your plants. Pour a half inch of water into the tray every few days. Keep containers from sitting in the water, to avoid root rot.

14. Watch for pests; if they appear, immediately isolate any infested plants to prevent the problem from spreading, and treat them with insecticidal soap or send them to the compost pile.

An Encyclopedia of Kitchen Herbs

The following is a detailed list of the most common culinary herbs. The basic cultural information about how to prepare the soil, planting techniques, seed starting, irrigation, mulching, fertilizing, pruning, and pest and disease control is covered in Appendixes A and B.

For each entry the common name of the herb is given as the title, followed by the herb's Latin name. The first word in a Latin name is the plant's genus, namely, a small group of plants that are closely related and similar to each other. The second name is the species. These are plants that are so closely related they are able to interbreed. When more than one species is being described in the entry they are designated as *spp.* It is critical to use the Latin name of unfamiliar edible plants as the common names of plants change from region to region and may be used to describe plants that are not edible, even ones that are toxic.

The herbs I have chosen to cover here are my favorites. Many of the herb entries include named cultivated varieties that are designated by single quotes. These select varieties (also known as cultivars) are most often available only from specialty herb nurseries. I have chosen them for their unusual foliage or flavor variations and I find them worth seeking out.

I have also included a number of exotic herbs. Some have there own unique flavors, others have tastes similar to familiar herbs and can be used as substitutes for the more common herbs in the warmest summer areas. To purchase the more unusual varieties you need to seek out specialty herb growers.

Oregano and Roman chamomile work well in the mixed border that lines my front walk. On my way into the house I can harvest a few sprigs of oregano for my supper.

ANGELICA
Angelica archangelica

Angelica is a large-leafed herb that grows up to 6 feet (app. 2 m) and more. In humid climates it can be a dramatic backdrop to a flower border. Both the aromatic leaves and the stems impart a slight anise flavor and are used in numerous savory dishes.

HOW TO GROW: Angelica is a biennial that produces huge clusters of creamy yellow flowers in the summer, beginning in its second year. It's amazingly hardy, to USDA Zone 3, but it grows very poorly in the Deep South. It is started from seeds in rich, well-drained, slightly acidic soil. Keep it fairly moist during the growing season, and apply nitrogen if the foliage starts to yellow. Aphids and stem rot are occasional problems. In arid climates it grows less rampantly than in humid ones.

HOW TO PREPARE: The fresh stems can be used sparingly to flavor salads. The stems can be preserved, most popularly by candying. To use the stems for candying, harvest them before they flower. The fresh leaves can also be used in salads and soups and cooked with fish or poultry. Angelica has been used to flavor liqueurs such as Chartreuse and vermouth for centuries.

ANISE
Pimpinella anisum

Since ancient times anise has been enjoyed for its slightly licorice taste.

HOW TO GROW: Anise is an annual plant started from seed in the garden. Thin seedlings to 6 inches (15 cm) apart. The plants grow to about 2 feet (0.6 m) and put out both lobed and feathery green leaves and umbels (flat flower heads that grow out from a central point) of cream-colored flowers. The ripe seeds are produced only in hot-summer areas. Anise is fussy about its growing

ABOVE: Angelica. BOTTOM: Anise

conditions and needs full sun and moist, well-drained soil. Pick the seed heads when they start to mature, clean them, and store them in a warm, dry place.

HOW TO PREPARE: The leaves can be used for seasoning soups or made into a tea, and the seeds are used in baked goods, including the traditional German *pfeffernuss* cookies, and sausages. Anise seeds can be used in place of caraway seeds in bread recipes. Anise is also used in liqueurs, salad dressings, and (my favorite way) spaghetti sauce and chicken cacciatore.

ANISE HYSSOP
Agastache foeniculum

An exception in the herb world, anise hyssop is native to the Western Hemisphere. Like artichokes, anise hyssop changes the chemical makeup of saliva, so subsequent foods tend to taste sweet.

Anise hyssop is also beautiful in a bouquet. Not only does it give us graceful spikes of lavender flowers, but it has a lovely aroma.

HOW TO GROW: This highly ornamental plant is an easily grown herbaceous perennial that reaches from 3–6 feet (1–2 m) and has gray-green leaves and striking, dense 1–3-inch (2.5–8 cm) flower spikes ranging from mauve to lavender to white. It is hardy to USDA Zone 4. Start anise hyssop from seeds or divisions and grow it in full sun in average soil, and keep it fairly moist. The plant dies down in the winter and often reseeds itself the next spring. It is bothered by few pests and diseases.

HOW TO PREPARE: The young leaves and tiny petals of the sweet flowers have a flavor somewhat between anise and root beer; the leaves and petals, if used sparingly, are very pleasant in salads, iced drinks, soups, tea breads, and desserts. Great with mushrooms, this is one of the tastiest of the edible flowers.

Anise Hyssop

BASIL
Ocimum basilicum

Basil is the herb most associated with Italy, yet it is native to Asia and Africa. It's a member of the mint family, and its aroma does in fact have "minty" overtones. There are different types of basil with familiar flavors, namely cinnamon, anise, and lemon, and different forms and foliage colors as well. (Someone calculated there were at least thirty varieties of basil available from specialty seed companies.)

HOW TO GROW: Basils are primarily annuals that glory in hot weather and will wither after a light frost. Gardeners in cool-summer areas struggle to keep basil going, as it needs many days in the eighties to grow well. Choose a well-drained area of the garden, in full sun or with a light amount of shade, where the soil is fairly fertile and has high amounts of organic matter. There are many basils to choose from. The familiar sweet basil is the most common and the most varied, as many purveyors have selected their own strains. You may want to buy sweet basil from different sources and see which ones you prefer. Variations

ABOVE FROM LEFT TO RIGHT: 'Green Ruffles' basil, 'Siam Queen' basil, Common basil, the heirloom 'Mrs. Burns' Famous Lemon Basil.

BOTTOM: 'African Blue,' 'Green Ruffles,' and 'Dark Opal' basil grow in a bed with 'Tabasco' pepper at the National Herb Garden in Washington

include the large-leafed 'Lettuce-Leaf' and 'Genovese' and the even larger-leafed 'Mammoth' sweet basils. I urge you to try the lemon-, cinnamon-, and anise-flavored varieties too. 'Anise' basil is a fairly large plant with purple-tinged foliage and has a strong aniselike aroma. 'Cinnamon' basil looks quite similar but has a perfumed cinnamon taste. The most dramatic basils, 'Red Rubin' and 'Purple Ruffles,' have deep purple foliage and pink flowers—great for coloring basil vinegar pink, but they make dreadful-looking brown

pesto. 'Siam Queen' and 'Queenette' are striking Thai basils with spicy flavor and compact purple flower heads. There are a number of dwarf basils with small leaves that when planted in a row will neatly edge a flower or vegetable bed. They are 'Fino Verde,' 'Green Globe,' 'Green Bouquet,' 'Piccolo,' and 'Spicy Globe.' All taste great as well. Try also the lemon-flavored varieties, 'Sweet Dani' and 'Mrs. Burns' Famous Lemon Basil'—both are much more vigorous than the standard lemon basil. If your family loves basil, plan for four to six plants of sweet basil to give you enough for pesto, and one or two of a number of scented varieties for flavoring and coloring salads, marinades, vinegars, and oils. Basil plants can be grown in a vegetable garden but are at home in the flower border as well, combined with petunias, zinnias, and dwarf marigolds. The purple varieties and some of the colorful scented basils are stylish among peppers and bush beans.

You can start basil seeds inside to plant out later, and the more common varieties are also available as transplants in many nurseries in the spring or summer. Basil put out in the garden before the weather is really warm will just sit there and suffer. When starting seeds, be aware that basil seeds are slippery and are easily washed out of the row if you don't water them gently. They will sprout in about seven to ten days. Thin seedlings to about a foot (30 cm) apart. If starting your seeds inside, plant them a month before the weather warms up. Transplant them out into the garden, spacing them about a foot (30 cm) apart. Keep the plants fairly moist during the growing season. If your soil is not very fertile, feed them every six weeks, making sure they have enough

nitrogen to keep the leaves quite green. If the leaves seem to pucker a lot (some is normal) and get small light yellow splotches, treat the plants with dolomite for a calcium deficiency.

You will be able to harvest leaves about eighty days from sowing and can usually continue until the first frost. Leaves may be picked or cut. If you don't keep the flower heads continually cut back, the plant will go to seed and give you few leaves. To further extend the season, bring in container-grown basil well before the first frost, or take sprigs off some of your garden plants and root them in water to keep them growing for a few months on a sunny windowsill. To keep your shoots vigorous, every so often add fertilizer to the water.

Basil is sometimes bothered by slugs and snails, as well as cucumber and Japanese beetles. Fusarium wilt is a growing problem; plants look healthy, and then either the whole plant or just a few branches start wilting and will not revive. Remove the plants and destroy them. Do not replant basil in the same soil for many consecutive years.

HOW TO PREPARE: The aromatic leaves of basil are best used fresh in many dishes—soups, salads, stews, and spaghetti sauce, to name a few. To many people, basil is best known as the base for pesto, an Italian herb sauce. To others, it is the "only" accompaniment to fresh, ripe tomatoes. In France it flavors the famous *soupe au pistou*, a Provençal vegetable soup. Basil vinegars and oils add their rich perfume to salads all over the Mediterranean. Thai basil is traditional for stir-fries, sauces for rice dishes, and added to a poke bowl. Hindus float the seeds on top of sweet drinks for their reputed cooling effect.

Bay laurel

CAUTION Pregnant and lactating women should avoid these as more than eight to ten flowers can cause milk to flow!

Borage

BAY LAUREL
(Sweet Bay, Grecian Laurel)
Laurus nobilis

The aromatic leaves of the bay tree have been used in cooking since Roman times. California bay (unrelated to sweet bay) is not considered culinary.

HOW TO GROW: Bay is a woody perennial. Purchase plants or grow them from seeds (you'll have a very long wait). Plant it in good, fast-draining soil. Bay laurel is not hardy, growing only to USDA Zone 8; in cold-winter areas plant it in containers and bring it inside to use as a houseplant. (Watch for scale insects, small shieldlike casings attached to the bark, and psyllids that deform the foliage. Treat both with refined horticultural oil if they appear. Look for the newly-introduced bay laurel 'Saratoga' which is resistant to the bay psyllid.) Harvest leaves as you need them. The leaves dry well and become sweeter when dried.

HOW TO PREPARE: The strong, almost resinous-tasting leaves of bay are used in soups, stews, spaghetti sauces, and marinades. The flavor is better if the bay leaf is added toward the end of cooking. Be sure to remove bay leaves from dishes before you serve them.

BORAGE
Borago officinalis

This herb is native to Europe and Africa and has a slight cucumber flavor.

HOW TO GROW: Borage is an easily grown summer annual that sometimes acts as a biennial. Borage plants grow to about 2 feet (0.6 m) and have hairy gray leaves and deep blue, ½-inch (13-mm) star-shaped flowers. The plants are easily started from seeds. Plant seeds in the spring in average soil and full sun after all threat of a frost is over. You can harvest young leaves once the plants are established, and flowers anytime they appear. Borage often reseeds itself.

HOW TO PREPARE: Young leaves can be added to salads, especially with cucumbers, and minced and added to soups. The 1-inch (2.5-cm) borage flowers can be used in salads, to garnish soups, or to decorate desserts. They can also be crystallized. To make flowers edible, you must remove the hairy sepals from the flowers using the following simple procedure. With your left hand (if you are right-handed) grasp the stem of the flower. With your right hand gently pinch the middle of the star and pull. The flower (corolla) should separate from the sepals intact.

Salad burnet

TOP AND BOTTOM: Caraway

BURNET, SALAD
Poterium sanguisorba

This attractive plant produces leaves with a slight cucumber taste.

HOW TO GROW: Salad burnet is an easily grown perennial plant hardy to USDA Zone 3. Its green leaves look divided and mostly sprout from the crown. Start this lovely little plant from seeds or divisions in the spring. Plant it in full or partial sun in poor soil, keep it fairly moist, and cut off seed heads as they appear (or they will reseed in the garden). Burnet has few pests or diseases.

HOW TO PREPARE: Harvest the young leaves and use them fresh in salads, as a garnish in summer drinks, and in sauces or vinegars. Burnet does not retain its flavor well when dried. For centuries Italians have gathered the young spring foliage of borage and salad burnet from the wild and added it to salads. Later in the season, when the leaves are more mature, they use them as a pot herb in combination with greens like spinach and chard in soups and risottos.

CARAWAY
Carum carvi

The pungent seeds of caraway are a favorite seasoning in parts of northern Europe.

HOW TO GROW: Caraway is a biennial that produces carrotlike leaves the first year and flower heads and seeds the second year. It's hardy to USDA Zone 4. Sow the seeds in spring in a sunny, well-drained soil and keep them fairly moist. If the soil freezes in the winter, mulch the plants well. Harvest the seed heads a month after they have blossomed. Shake the heads into a paper bag and separate the seeds from the debris. Store them in a warm, dry place.

HOW TO PREPARE: Caraway seeds give a distinctive flavor to many dishes. Add to vegetables, salads, rye breads, sauerkraut, and stuffed cabbage.

CHAMOMILE
Chamaemelum nobile; Matricaria recutita

There are two types of chamomile: the perennial type, which is low-growing and moderately hardy, and an annual chamomile, which is a lovely short-lived garden flower.

HOW TO GROW: The annual chamomile, *matricaria recutita*, sometimes called German chamomile, grows to about 18 inches (46 cm) and produces a cloud of small white daisies. It has a sweeter taste, is less medicinal, and is preferred by many for making tea over the perennial chamomile. Start both chamomiles from seed in well-prepared soil in full sun. Keep it fairly moist. Or plant perennial chamomile from plants available from the nursery. It is hardy to USDA Zone 4. Both are quite free of most pests and diseases.

HOW TO PREPARE: Most cooks prefer the flavor of the annual chamomile. The perennial is most often used for medicinal purposes. Use the flower heads fresh or dried in herbal teas, and the petals in salads. The heads dry well for winter use.

German chamomile

Chervil

CHERVIL
Anthriscus cerefolium

This delicate, lacy-looking herb is used quite commonly in France. Its slightly anise flavor is a favorite in salads and sauces. Chervil is also one of the herbs that make up the traditional herbal mixture *fines herbes*.

HOW TO GROW: Chervil is an annual herb that grows best in cool weather; because it doesn't transplant well, it is generally sown in place in early spring and again in fall. Give the plants morning or filtered sun and rich soil, and keep them well watered. Chervil seeds need light to germinate. Plant seeds in shallow furrows a ½ inch (13 mm) deep and cover the furrows with damp cheesecloth. Keep the cheesecloth damp until the seeds germinate. Thin the seedlings to 6–12 inches (15–30 cm) apart. Begin to harvest sprigs when the plants are 6 inches (15 cm) tall. The plants are short-lived, so, as with radishes and lettuces, to keep a supply, sow seeds every few weeks during the cool part of the spring and fall. In some climates if you allow the plants to go to seed, they reseed themselves.

HOW TO PREPARE: Chervil wilts readily, so harvest it fresh as close to preparation time as possible. The delicate anise-flavored leaves of chervil are used fresh in salads, with eggs and salmon, in cream soups, in cream- and goat-cheese spreads, and chopped and added at the last minute to many classic sauces. It is hard to preserve the delicate flavor of chervil. Drying destroys its flavor; instead make a chervil butter and freeze it for up to two months.

CHIVES
Allium spp.

Chives are enjoyed by the herb sophisticate as well as the beginner, and they are so easy to grow that I sometimes refer to them as the herb with built-in training wheels. They also must be the easiest herb to cook with, as they enhance any dish suitable for onions.

HOW TO GROW: There are two types of culinary chives. *A. schoenoprasum*, sometimes called onion chives, has a mild onion flavor, tubular grasslike leaves from twelve to 18 inches (46 cm) high, and globe-shaped lavender flowers. The second type of chives, *A. tuberosum*, Chinese or garlic chives, is a distant relative and has an onion/garlic flavor, flat leaves from 18–24 inches (46–61 cm) tall, and white star-shaped flowers. Both are perennial plants hardy to USDA Zone 3. Onion chives are worldly plants native to most of the Northern Hemisphere; Chinese chives are native to Asia.

Both types of chives need at least six hours of sun a day, and average to rich, well-drained, moist soil. Chives are best planted in spring and can be

Garlic or Chinese chives

obtained as divisions, purchased as transplants, or grown from seeds. Richters Herbs (www.richters.com) carries a few specialized varieties of onion chives, namely, 'Grolau,' bred for greenhouse and growing indoors, and 'Profusion,' a variety bred for its flowers, which remain edible for an extended time because they don't set seeds, a process that makes the flowers papery and inedible.

Plant onion chives in the front of, or as a border to, your herb or flower beds and in the vegetable garden. Chinese chives, as they are taller, look best interplanted among other herbs and flowers. Both types of chives grow well in containers. Plant them alone or combine them with other herbs such as thyme and parsley.

To keep chives growing well, apply nitrogen fertilizer in the spring or if leaves are yellow. In rainy areas supplemental watering is seldom needed, and pests (except for occasional aphids) and diseases are few and far between. Once your chive plants are a few months old, you can harvest them from spring through fall by cutting the leaves an inch above the crown of the plant.

Trim chives occasionally, as they can reseed and become a nuisance, especially the Chinese ones.

Onion chives

Cut them back after flowering, and they will soon look new again. Divide your plants every three or four years to renew them.

HOW TO PREPARE: Tasting as they do of onions, both types of chives are used whenever a mild onion flavor is needed in a salad, say, or in sauces, dips, and marinades. They can be substituted in recipes calling for scallions or be made into chive butter to melt over vegetables or combined with sour cream and cream or goat cheeses. Shower baked or mashed potatoes, creamy or clear soups, and omelets with chopped chives. The flower petals of the onion chives are pleasantly crunchy when young, but fibrous and papery when mature. Pull apart the lavender florets and sprinkle them on your food as you would the leaves. Chinese chive leaves can be used chopped in stir-fries and dumplings, soups and Thai curries. There are special varieties available through Asian specialty seed companies. After blanching them, you can eat the resulting tender stalks and buds as you would a vegetable. Though not as tasty as fresh, both types of chives can be dried or frozen, either whole or chopped, or made into butters or preserved in vinegar.

CILANTRO
(fresh coriander)
Coriandrum sativum

This pungent herb looks something like parsley, but its taste is very different. It has an earthy flavor some people dislike strongly and others (like me) crave.

Known in the cooking of the Americas as cilantro, or even Chinese parsley, this herb is referred to as coriander in Asia. Whether you call it cilantro or coriander, this herb is among the most popular in the world.

There are other herbs with this same seductive flavor, those Carole Saville calls cilantro mimics. They are culantro (*Eryngium foetidum*) and papaloquelite (*Porophyllum ruderale* subsp. *macrocephalum*), both native to the Americas, and rau ram (*Polygonum odoratum*), also known as Vietnamese

Cilantro

coriander. All grow best in warm weather, in the eighties, and can take little frost. Papaloquelite is an annual; the others are tender perennials. The first two can be started from seeds; rau ram is started from cuttings. The cilantro mimics are available from a few specialty herb nurseries.

HOW TO GROW: The standard cilantro is an easily grown annual herb that grows best in cool weather. (Some nurseries sell seedlings in six plants or so to a small 4-inch (about 10 cm) container. Gently separate the young plants and plant them out.

Cilantro bolts to seed readily when the days start to lengthen and in warm weather. Therefore, it is best planted in late summer/early fall in all climates. In cold-winter areas the seeds will sprout the next spring after the ground thaws, and in mild-winter areas the plants will grow lush and tall. (Cilantro tolerates light frosts.) In short-spring areas early plantings are more successful than later ones. One guaranteed way to grow under these conditions is to treat cilantro as a cut-and-come-

NOTE Herbs such as dill, fennel, caraway, and cilantro (coriander) produce seeds that are added to cooked dishes. For the most flavor, before using these seeds toast them in a dry frying pan over low heat until they just begin to perfume the air. Toasting brings out the flavor of the seeds and adds a nuttiness to the final dish.

Cilantro picked with the roots intact

HOW TO PREPARE: Cilantro leaves are almost always used raw, as the flavor fades quickly when they are cooked. Generally they are chopped and sprinkled on a dish or mixed in after cooking to give it a distinct flavor. In many Asian and South American dishes cilantro is among the most important flavoring and the sometimes-recommended parsley is not a suitable substitute. There is no successful way to preserve the flavor of cilantro because it fades very quickly once the essential oils are exposed to the air.

Add the leaves sparingly to salads, guacamole, Korean bibimbap and stir-fries, fold them into cooked vegetable dishes and salsa, or use whole leaves as a garnish on Asian soups and in tacos, burritos, and quesadillas. Or, try them in a vegan Moroccan pesto of cilantro, parsley and cumin. The herbs most often used with cilantro are the many oreganos. Seasonings that complement cilantro are ginger, garlic, and cumin. The seeds of cilantro, called coriander seeds, can be harvested, dried, and used to season curries, cookies, and rice dishes. The seeds are most flavorful if they are toasted in a dry frying pan for a few minutes before you grind them with a mortar and pestle or in a spice grinder. Coriander (cilantro) roots are a favored seasoning in Southeast Asia, especially Thailand. They taste like a mellow cilantro. Plants grown under optimum cool temperatures in rich soil produce roots large enough to be satisfying. Chop the roots to use in stir-fries or to make a popular Thai green curry paste, and pound the roots with garlic and black pepper to use as a base to season numerous Thai dishes. In recipes that call for coriander root, you may substitute cilantro stems instead.

again crop and plant seeds an inch apart and snip seedlings at ground level when they're 3 inches (8 cm) tall; then replant every two weeks until the weather gets too warm.

Starting cilantro by seed is easy and more successful than transplanting. Plant seeds a quarter inch deep in rich, light soil and in full sun. Thin the seedlings to 4–6 inches (10–15 cm) apart. Keep the seedlings moist to ensure lush growth. The varieties most commonly available in nurseries, while adequate, are specifically grown for the world seed trade; their seeds are used as a spice called coriander. However, you can grow varieties selected for leaf production, such as 'Chinese,' 'Long Standing,' and 'Slo-Bolt,' available from numerous online seed companies. Harvest the sprigs once plants are 6 inches (15 cm) tall. Fertilize the plants only if they get pale. Cilantro has few pests and diseases. When the roots are needed for a recipe, harvest whole, mature plants using a spading fork. First loosen the soil well around the roots so they won't break off in the ground. Cilantro flowers, tiny flat sprays of white petals, are also edible, as well as great for attracting beneficial insects to your garden.

DILL
Anethum graveolens

Dill is a European herb famous in pickles, but it's also quite versatile and enjoyable in many different dishes. Both the young leaves and the seeds are used.

HOW TO GROW: Start these annual plants in the spring from seeds after the weather has warmed up. Plant them in full sun in well-drained, fertile soil. Make successive sowings for a continuous supply of fresh leaves. These ferny plants have flat sprays of yellow flowers and grow to 3 feet (1 m), so give them room to spread. Keep dill moist throughout the growing season and harvest the leaves as soon as the plants get 4–5 inches (10–12 cm) tall. Save the seed heads and dry them in a warm, dry place. The varieties 'Dukat' ('Tetra-dill'), 'Fernleaf,' and 'Bouquet' are shorter and more vigorous than the standard dill offered in nurseries.

HOW TO PREPARE: Use dill leaves fresh in salads; omelets; vegetable dishes, especially with spinach, carrots, beets, and potatoes; and fish sauces and with mild soft cheeses. Use the seeds in pickling cucumbers, snap beans, carrots, and beets. Preserve the leaves of dill by drying them or putting them in vinegar or oil. Harvest the seeds, dry them, and keep them in a cool, dry place.

NOTE: Dill, fennel, chervil, parsley, and caraway are all members of the same botanical family, the Apiaceae. This family produces flat sprays of small flowers that are especially attractive to beneficial insects. As a bonus, the flowers are also edible and can be broken into small florets and added to salads or used as a garnish.

FENNEL
Foeniculum vulgare

This herb has beautiful, ferny foliage and a flavor reminiscent of licorice. It is favored in some cultures as a digestive.

HOW TO GROW: Though a perennial, fennel is usually grown as you would dill. Cut plants back in spring to keep the plant looking trim. A coppery-colored fennel variety called 'Rubrum' (bronze) is striking in the landscape. Keep the seed heads removed, as fennel will reseed and become a weed in many parts of the country. Fennel is a favorite food of the swallowtail butterfly larvae.

HOW TO PREPARE: The leaves can be used in salads, sauces, soups, stews, omelets, and salad dressings, and on fish and pasta. Throw the dry plant prunings onto the barbecue when you are grilling fish for a great rich flavor. Or use them to spice up an apple shrub. Use the seeds in spaghetti, soups, sauerkraut, and bread pudding. Preserve it as you would dill. Online you can find recipes using fennel pollen, for instance in shortbread cookies.

'Fernleaf' dill

'Rubrum' fennel

HOPS
Humulus lupulus

Hops are sprawling perennial herbaceous vines best known for producing flowers that add aroma and bitterness to beer. Their cone-like blooms are covered with yellow glands that contain the prized aromatic bitters called lupulin. Historically aromatic herbs were added to beer not only for flavor but also because they have an antibacterial effect on microbes that could spoil the beer.

HOW TO GROW: A single female plant will provide all the hops (female flowers) you need for most home brewing. This fast-growing, herbaceous perennial vine (actually called a bine) can attain 25 feet (about 7.5 m) in a season, and because they grow vertically and rampantly they need a strong arbor or fence. The shoots wind clockwise and cling with hooked hairs. To train them to grow horizontally, hand-guide the stem tips.

Hops grow just about anywhere except in desert areas. Order your shoots or plants in spring. The vine requires full sun and humus-rich, well-drained soil (pH between 6 and 7). Work compost and a balanced organic fertilizer into the planting hole; plant bare-root divisions 1 inch (2.5 cm) deep, bud side up, the plants at soil level. If growing more than one, space plants 6 feet (about 2 m) apart. Provide plenty of water once they sprout in spring. Hops rarely bloom the first year, and die back to the crown every autumn.

Every spring thin out the new shoots as soon as they appear or you'll soon have a tangle of vines. (Hop shoots are edible and considered a delicacy in hop growing areas. The tender spring shoots look like thin, branched asparagus and are slightly bitter. You need a lot for a meal. To prepare, snap off the top 6 inches (15 cm) of the shoot, cook, and serve as you would asparagus. When boiling hop shoots, add lemon juice to prevent discoloration.) Leave the 4–6 most vigorous shoots to grow. Fertilize in early summer. Pick hops mid-August to September, depending on the variety and weather. At maturity, hops develop a drier, papery feel and

Hops

lighten in color. Clip off the clusters. In fall, cut the vines back to ground level; mulch well to protect from winter freezing.

Downy mildew can be a problem in rainy spring climates; powdery mildew is primarily a problem in the Northeast; and mites can build up in hot, dry climates. To prevent mildews, plant resistant varieties, carefully strip the leaves off the bottom 3 or 4 feet (about 1–1.25 m) of the vines to improve air circulation, and clean up all dead leaves and dispose of them in the fall.

Purchase bare-root divisions of female shoots or plants in early spring from Raintree Nursery, The Thyme Garden Herb Company, Great Lakes Hops, (the largest producer), and Nichols Garden Nursery, which also sells beer making supplies. If they arrive too early for planting, keep them moist and refrigerated. Some states prohibit hop plant imports. In that case, locate an herb nursery in your state.

There are two types of hop cultivars: bittering (adds bitter flavors to beer) and aroma (imparts smell and taste to beer and are the best shoots for eating). Catalogs often include alpha percentages; higher numbers indicate more bittering compounds. Beer flavors vary with the cultivars used, some are floral, spicy, citrusy, and/or earthy. When choosing varieties for your garden, select for taste and the intended use you prefer. Varieties include: 'Cascade', a popular all-purpose strain in many American light lagers; 'Kent Golding' is a traditional English aroma type hop for ales and lagers with a delicate flavor; 'Mt. Hood' is an aroma type with a mild flavor for Bavarian-style lagers; 'Nugget' is a vigorous, bittering type for ales and stouts that resists downy mildew, and 'Willamette', an aroma-type hybrid for English-style ales; spicy aroma. It is resistant to downy mildew.

HOW TO PREPARE: Making your own beer is legal in all fifty states and most countries. If you are new to brewing check locally to see if nearby breweries give classes and sell brewing supplies. Check also online for websites that can guide you through the process. In addition there are numerous books on the topic. I especially recommend *The Homebrewers Garden, 2nd edition* Storey Publishing 2016) not only for how to brew but for growing your own malt grains and brewing herbs.

To prepare your hops for brewing, first dry them in a shady warm area or in a food dehydrator until papery. Quality deteriorates quickly; freeze in heavy-duty zipper bags or sealable glass jars and use within 6 months. Hops yield ½ to 2 pounds (.25–1 k) of dried flowers per plant.

LAVENDER
(English, aka French)
Lavandula angustifolia (officinalis)

The scent of lavender is among the most treasured scents in the Western world. Few folks think of feasting with it, and so many miss the opportunity to enjoy it to a fuller extent.

HOW TO GROW: Lavender plants grow to a height of 2–3 feet (0.6–1 m) and are hardy to USDA Zone 5. The foliage of most lavenders is gray and the flowers are lavender. Start lavender from cuttings or transplants and plant them in full sun. One variety 'Lavender Lady', readily starts from seeds and, unlike most lavenders, will bloom the first year. Watering is usually needed only in arid climates and when the plant is grown in containers, and then only when the soil is fairly dry. Shear the plants back after they bloom. Like most of the Mediterranean herbs, lavender does poorly in heavy or poorly drained soil and will succumb to root rot readily. In hot weather, lavenders occasionally become infested with spider mites.

HOW TO PREPARE: There are many species of lavender. The English/French is the culinary one. With the strong lemon-perfume taste of the petals of its 2-inch (5-cm) flower heads, lavender is one of the most useful culinary flowers. Leaves and flower heads can be steeped for use in drinks, jellies, soufflés, sorbets, and ice cream. Use the petals sparingly in salads and soups, and as a garnish. Lavender buds are one of the ingredients in the herb blend known as *herbes de Provence*.

English lavender

LEMONGRASS
Cymbopogon citratus

An aromatic grass-family herb with a rich lemon flavor, lemongrass is much prized in Southeast Asia.

HOW TO GROW: Native to the tropics, lemongrass can be grown outdoors in very mild climates and in containers in cold ones, and then brought inside for the winter. It's hardy into the mid-20s °F (app. -4°C) Purchase divisions from local nurseries and some specialty seed companies. (Sometimes stalks from the grocery store will root.) Plant the divisions in good, well-draining soil, in part shade. Fertilize the plants a few times during the growing season and keep the soil moist. Lemongrass has few disease and pest problems.

HOW TO PREPARE: Harvest the white leafstalks at the base of the lemongrass plant once it's established and use it as a seasoning in Thai dishes; sparingly in light soups; in marinades and fish and chicken dishes; and as a wonderful refreshing tea. Mash the stalk before use, to release the oils when putting it in a soup, and mince it very fine if you're using lemongrass in a salad or stir-fry. When you use it whole, remove the lemongrass stalk from the dish before serving.

To preserve lemongrass, either dry it or freeze the fleshy stalks.

LEMON VERBENA
Aloysia triphylla

Lemon verbena is another tropical herb with a strong lemon flavor.

HOW TO GROW: This woody perennial shrub grows to 10 feet (3 m) in mild-winter areas and is hardy to about 10°F (-12.2°C). In most areas it will lose its leaves in winter. In cold-winter areas it can be grown in containers and brought inside or grown in a greenhouse. Plants brought inside will lose their leaves and should be kept in a fairly cool place. Cut the plant back and repot it in early spring.

Purchase plants or start them from seeds. Starting from seeds is a slow process. In mild climates situate plants in a sunny area of the garden in good soil. Lemon verbena produces sprays of tiny white flowers in summer. Prune it often to keep the plant looking trim. Once plants are a foot (30 cm) or so tall, harvest the leaves throughout the growing season.

HOW TO PREPARE: Use the lemon flavor of this herb in fruit salads, jellies, and fruit drinks, as a tea or garnish, and with chicken or fish. The leaves dry well and retain their flavor.

Lemongrass and lemon verbena both contain the same primary chemical, citral, that gives them their "citrusy" flavor. The herbs can be used interchangeably in recipes, but both plants contain other flavorful chemicals as well, so the flavor of the final dish will have a subtle difference.

Lemongrass

Lemon verbena and purple echinacea

Lovage

MINT
Mentha spp.

Mints have that familiar clean and clear taste. The Egyptians, Greeks, Romans, and other cultures throughout Europe and Asia have used mint to flavor foods for eons.

HOW TO GROW: Mints are perennial plants, and most are hardy to USDA Zone 5, grow to 2 feet (0.6 m) tall, have shiny green leaves, and are quite rangy. If not controlled, most can become invasive. Mints spread by underground runners, so they are best planted in containers or within rings of metal flashing in the ground to contain the roots. There are many different kinds of mint. Among the most commonly used culinary ones are spear-

Spearmint and lemon balm

LOVAGE
Levisticum officinale

This large European herb has a strong flavor reminiscent of celery.

HOW TO GROW: Lovage is a perennial hardy to USDA Zone 3, but it is usually treated as an annual in hot, humid climates. Start seeds in the garden in late summer or fall. In the coldest areas start it inside and plant it out once the weather warms in spring. Plant lovage in full sun or partial shade in moist soil with good drainage. In moist areas the plant can grow to 6 feet (app. 2 m), so give it lots of room and keep seed heads cut off, or the plant will reseed itself. Harvest young leaves once the plants are a foot (30 cm) high. Collect seed heads and dry them in a cool, dry place.

HOW TO PREPARE: Use the young leaves sparingly in salads, soups, and stews, or with meat and poultry dishes. Chopped young stems can be used as you would celery. The stems can be candied, like angelica, frozen for winter use, or used in a *bouquet garni*. The seeds can be used to flavor pickles, soups, and baked goods.

mint, peppermint, apple mint, and pineapple mint. Rewarding for gardeners and cooks are the unusual, but easily grown, 'Grapefruit' mint, 'Orange' mint, 'Pineapple' mint, 'Mint the Best,' 'Curly' mint, 'Chocolate' mint, 'Lavender' mint, 'Persian' mint, and the very close relative lemon balm.

Nepitella, *Calamintha nepeta*, is another relative. There are other plants referred to as nepitella but calamint is the one most commonly available. It has a mint flavor with overtones of apple and thyme. The plant has small green leaves and pink or white flowers on small spikes. In Italy nepitella is used with mushrooms, eggplant, and in potato dishes.

> **CAUTION** Evidence indicates that nepitella should be avoided by pregnant women.

Most mints prefer moist, sunny to partly sunny conditions. Set out the plants in the spring; once they are growing vigorously, they can be harvested anytime throughout the year. Prune heavily two or three times a year to keep plants under control. Under some conditions mints are prone to whitefly infestation. Cut the plant back and spray with a soap-based pesticide. Rust is another problem that can infest mint. If you have a serious infestation of either, pull the plant out and start with new plants somewhere else in the garden. Mints bloom in midsummer. The flowers in some varieties are white; in others, lavender to violet. Cut off the seed heads of lemon balm, or it can seed itself and be a nuisance.

HOW TO PREPARE: All the mints have a characteristic clean "minty" flavor. In addition, lemon balm has a citrus taste. The leaves are best used fresh, though they can be preserved by freezing and drying. They are famous in mint julep and mojitos—and mint tea. Use them in cool drinks, in green salads, in Middle Eastern dishes such as tabouli, with cucumbers, in soups, and in savory sauces, particularly with mustard or garlic served with lamb. Popular in Southeast Asia, mints are used in salads, curries, and soups. Also try mint in sweet dishes—desserts, jellies, sauces, fruit salads, and, of course, with chocolate.

OREGANO AND MARJORAM
various spp.

When you think of oregano, think of its flavor, not the plant. There are a number of unrelated plants that have the essential oil—carvacrol—that gives all oregano-type plants the characteristic taste cooks favor. One of the most flavorful European oreganos is 'Greek' oregano, Origanum vulgare subspecies *hirtum*, a native to the Mediterranean, though sometimes this herb is used interchangeably with its close relative, Italian oregano, *O. x majoricum*. However, in much of South America and the Caribbean the term oregano usually refers to different and unrelated plants. *Plectranthus amboinicus*, Cuban oregano, and *Lippia graveolens* and *Poliomentha longiflora*, two Mexican oreganos, also smell and taste like oregano. To further confuse the oregano issue, the identification of good culinary European

'Greek' oregano

Mexican oregano

oreganos is difficult because of mislabeled and misidentified plants in nurseries. As Carole Saville says, "The key to the puzzle is your palate. If you find a plant at the nursery simply labeled 'oregano,' be suspicious." Taste it and see if it has a pleasant, spicy flavor before you purchase it. Herb mavens usually look for plants labeled 'Greek' oregano (*O. v.* subspecies *hirtum*, synonym *O. v. heracleoticum*) to find the best flavor. Sweet marjoram is another puzzle, as plants sold as sweet marjoram sometimes are really Italian oregano. Again, taste a leaf. Real sweet marjoram has a savory, sweet, pungent aroma and a taste of new-mown hay. If it is in bloom, you will notice that the buds look like little knots, hence the common name knotted marjoram.

It came as a surprise to me that the European oreganos are extremely high in antioxidants.

HOW TO GROW: The European oreganos are rangy perennials native to the arid mountainsides of the eastern Mediterranean. Common and 'Greek' oregano are hardy to USDA Zone 5, but sweet marjoram can't withstand hard frosts and is often grown as a summer annual. All must be planted in full sun in a light, fast-draining soil. To ensure the best flavor, start plants from transplants, cuttings, or divisions, not seeds. Cut plants back in late spring to encourage new growth and once again in midsummer to prevent them from becoming woody. Except in very sandy soils or in containers, moderate watering and little or no fertilizing will keep plants healthy. Root rots are a common problem in clay soils and in containers. Spider mites are occasional problems in hot weather and when plants are grown inside. Oreganos do poorly under hot, humid conditions and are treated as summer annuals in areas where the temperatures are regularly in the high eighties and above. Here, Cuban oregano, while very frost-sensitive, basks in the heat and humidity of summer. This handsome plant is related to coleus, grows to 2 feet (0.6 m) tall, and has large, fleshy green leaves. The variegated form has white margins. The two Mexican oreganos are hardy only to USDA Zone 9, and both are fairly tall woody plants with a rangy growth habit.

HOW TO PREPARE: The European oreganos are most commonly associated with a number of Italian sauces used with pizza, spaghetti, and marinades. They can also be used in soups, stews, salads, and most meat dishes. Unlike many herbs, European oreganos and sweet marjoram may be enjoyed both fresh and dried. I use them fresh when I want a mild, clean taste, and dry when I want a little more bite and an intense flavor. For traditional uses of the Mexican oreganos, add the dried leaves to chili dishes and salsa; to fillings for burritos, tamales, and chiles rellenos; and as sea-

soning in such seafood dishes as stuffed fish and ceviche, and meat dishes such as pork stew and tripe soup. In some parts of Mexico the leaves are toasted before use. All oreganos but the Cuban oregano can be air-dried by hanging the cuttings in a warm, dry place or dried in a dehydrator or the microwave oven. They may also be preserved in vinegar.

PARSLEY
Petroselinum crispum

Parsley is a versatile and nutritious herb whose leaves are used in most of the world's cuisines in one form or another. There are two major types—the curly one is best for garnishing, and the tall, flat-leafed type often called Italian parsley is used primarily for cooking because of its deep flavor

Sweet margoram (in pot) and curly parsley

and sweetness. All of the parsleys are high in antioxidants.

HOW TO GROW: Parsleys are biennials generally treated as annuals. The curly types have dark green, curly, finely divided leaves and are neat and tidy-looking in the garden. They seldom grow more than a foot (30 cm) tall and are useful to form borders, to use in the front of herb and flower gardens, and they combine well with flowering plants in containers. Varieties include 'Frisca Curly,' 'Extra Curled Dwarf,' 'Green River,' 'Triplecurled,' 'Mosscurled,' and 'Krausa.' Flat-leaf or Italian parsley grows to 2 feet (0.6 m) tall and is a somewhat rangy plant suitable for the middle of the herb border or in a vegetable garden. It's the preferred culinary parsley worldwide. Varieties include 'Gigante d' Italia' ('Giant Italian'), 'Catalogno,' and 'Single-Leaf' parsley. Standard curly parsley is used for flavoring and as a garnish.

Start seeds in the spring or buy plants from nurseries to set out. The plants do best in full sun and in rich, organic soil high in organic matter. Gardeners in the Deep South or in the western parts of USDA Zones 9 and 10 will have more success with parsley as a fall and winter plant. Parsley seeds take from two weeks up to a month to germinate. They will germinate more quickly if soaked in water for a few hours or if frozen in ice cubes for a few days. Don't let the seed bed dry out. Fertilize parsley midseason with nitrogen. Parsley will develop root rot problems in heavy or soggy soil, and it is the favored food for swallow-tail butterfly larvae.

The flavor of parsley fades when the herb is dried. Some gardeners in cold climates grow parsley in a sunny window over the winter.

HOW TO PREPARE: Harvest the outer leaves of parsley during the growing season. They are best used fresh, though they will retain some of their flavor when frozen or made into a butter. All parsleys are high in iron and vitamin C. This herb's refreshing, peppery flavor is compatible

Flat-leaf, or Italian parsley

with most herbs. And to add complexity of flavor as well as to sneak in extra nutrition, I always add it to marinaras and meat sauces and seldom make a soup, casserole, or stew without it. Parsley can stand alone when its leaves are chopped up and served with new potatoes, added to quinoa salad or tabouli.

Flat-leaf parsley is one of the most popular herbs in Italy. *Soffrito* is a traditional base for soups, stews, stir-fries, and pasta sauces made from onions, celery, carrots, and lots of flat-leaf parsley sautéed in a little olive oil, and in Argentina for chimichurri sauce.

ROSEMARY
Rosmarinus officinalis

Rosemary is a pungent, resinous herb native to the Mediterranean. Over the years it has become one of my favorite herbs, and at any one time I must have four or five different types growing in my garden. Its health benefits include stimulating the immune system, improving digestion, and reducing inflammation.

HOW TO GROW: Rosemary is a tender perennial grown from cuttings, divisions, and occasionally from seed. It needs full sun and fast-draining soil. In mild, arid climates it is so lovely, reliable, and versatile that it is used as a landscaping plant. Prostrate varieties spill over retaining walls and down hillsides; upright ones are used as trimmed or informal hedges and in mixed, drought-tolerant borders. In areas USDA Zone 8 and colder, it is usually grown as an annual or enjoyed in containers and brought inside for the winter. Most varieties of rosemary produce a profusion of light blue flowers in the spring and then a sprinkling of flowers throughout the summer. The form of the plant can vary from strongly upright to completely prostrate. The standard culinary rosemary has the light blue flowers. 'Arp' rosemary is reputed to be the hardiest rosemary, hardy to 10°F (-12°C); 'Miss Jessup's Upright' and 'Tuscan Blue' have unusually straight, woody stems, perfect for using as a flavorful skewer for barbecued meats and vegetables. 'Irene' and 'Tuscan Blue' have dark blue flowers, and 'Majorca Pink' has pink ones. 'Prostratus' is compact and trailing, great for containers and to grow over retaining walls. You can purchase many

ABOVE: 'Tuscan Blue' rosemary
LEFT: 'Prostratus' and 'Arp' rosemary

of the unusual varieties from specialty herb nurseries, both retail and online. Gardeners everywhere will have trouble with root rot if the soil drainage is poor, and spider mites are occasional problems when the weather is hot or the plants are grown inside. Gardeners in the South may have problems with nematodes and may be forced to grow rosemary in containers.

HOW TO PREPARE: The leaves can be harvested anytime during the growing season, though they will be most flavorful just before flowering. The flowers are edible and make a lovely confetti to sprinkle over salads and vegetable dishes. Preserve rosemary by drying or preserving it in vinegar or oil (see page 76). Rosemary lends its pinelike flavor to many dishes containing pork, veal, and lamb and is a favorite herb to add to soups, stews, breads or biscuits, and pizza toppings. Try it in marinades with garlic for grilling eggplant and mushrooms, or roast potatoes in the oven with olive oil, garlic, and rosemary. Use this herb sparingly, as the flavor is very strong.

SAFFRON
Crocus sativus

Probably one of the world's most expensive flavorings, saffron is the dried, pulverized stigmas of a fall-blooming crocus.

HOW TO GROW: Plant the corms of these crocuses in late summer. They are available from a few specialty seed companies and nurseries. Hardy to USDA Zone 6, these plants prefer rich, well-drained soil with some afternoon shade. Plant these pretty, mauve to purple crocuses in large quantities if you wish to harvest them for the saffron, because you'll need a lot of plants to yield a sufficient harvest. Divide and replant every two years.

HOW TO PREPARE: Remove the orange stigmas with tweezers, dry them for a few days, and store them in a covered jar in a warm, dry place. Grind and use them in rice dishes, including paella, with seafoods, and in East Indian dishes.

Saffron

CAUTION Do not confuse this crocus with the autumn crocus, *Colchicum*, which is poisonous.

ABOVE: Three sages: 'Berggarten,' 'Icterina,' and 'Tricolor'

SAGE
Salvia officinalis

Sage is a popular, pungent herb best known for its use in the stuffing for Thanksgiving turkey, but it is also great with potatoes or sausages and in stews. It is a powerful antioxidant as well as an powerful inflammatory.

HOW TO GROW: Most culinary sages are perennials that can be grown from cuttings or seeds. Common sage and most of its cultivars are hardy to USDA Zone 4 if given protection in the coldest regions. The purple, tricolor, and pineapple sages are hardy only to USDA Zone 7. Most sages do poorly in hot, humid climates and are treated as annuals in the Deep South. Plant sages in average soil, in full sun, and in soil with extremely good drainage. Sages die readily in heavy clay or if their roots stay damp. In hot weather, and with house-grown sages, spider mites are an occasional problem. Plants range in height from 2–4 feet (0.6–1.2 m). Numerous sages can be used in landscaping situations, in traditional herb gardens, and in containers. Most have gray foliage and purple flowers, but some have variegated foliage in colors of yellow, green, pink, and white. To keep these plants looking neat, trim them back once heavily in spring and, if they are leggy, again in summer. Garden sage is the most commonly used culinary variety. It has gray-green leaves and lavender flowers. 'Berggarten' is a robust sage with striking,

ABOVE: Garden sage
LEFT: 'Berggarten' sage

large, oval gray leaves. Golden sage, 'Icterina,' while colorful in the garden, is somewhat less preferred in the kitchen and does not bloom. Purple sage, 'Purpurascens,' has soft, aromatic purple leaves and purple flowers. Pineapple sage, *S. elegans*, which is propagated only by cuttings or divisions, grows to 4 feet (1.2 m) tall and produces spikes of bright red flowers that are loved by hummingbirds.

HOW TO PREPARE: The leaves of common garden sage are a favorite seasoning for all types of poultry, stuffings, sausages, and fish, as well as in soup, stews, cheeses, saltimbocca, and tomato sauces. Try adding sage when you roast potatoes. A famous Italian dish is baked white beans with garlic and sage. The flowers of all the sages that bloom are edible and can be sprinkled over salads, and the spikes of common sage are great dipped in a tempura batter and deep-fried. The leaves of pineapple sage have a distinctive pineapple taste and are used for teas and cold drinks and in fruit salads, jams, jellies, and salsas. The flowers can be used in fruit salads too and as garnish for pastries. Dried, the leaves of garden sage retain their flavor well, but the oils tend to get rancid, so for long storage, refrigerate or freeze.

SAVORY
Satureja spp.

Summer and winter savories are favored herbs from the Mediterranean. The most popular savory for culinary purposes is summer savory, called the bean herb in Germany.

HOW TO GROW: Summer savory is an easily grown annual plant that reaches 18 inches (46 cm) in height. It has very small gray-green leaves and small lavender to white flowers that bloom all summer long. Use the plants in a flower border, in containers, or in an herb garden. Start seeds in spring ⅛ inch (3–4 mm) deep in good soil in a sunny area. Keep both the seed bed and the ensuing plants moist. Harvest the herb once the plants are 6 inches (15 cm) tall.

Winter savory is a perennial that grows from six to 18 inches (46 cm) tall. It has compact, bright

Summer savory

green foliage and tiny spikes of white flowers, and it makes a handsome plant in the garden. There is a graceful creeping savory, *S. repandra*, that spills out of containers and can be used as a small-area ground cover. Winter savory, while slow to germinate, can be started from seeds, but it is usually propagated by cuttings or division. It is hardy to USDA Zone 6 and grows slowly. Plant it in full sun in sandy soil, and keep the plants somewhat moist during the growing season. Prune it in spring and again midsummer in mild climates, to keep it from becoming woody.

HOW TO PREPARE: Summer savory can be harvested throughout the summer and is best used fresh. Winter savory can be harvested throughout the season and is somewhat more successful preserved for winter use by freezing or drying. Better yet, keep the plant in a container and bring it inside for the winter. Savory adds a richness to foods. I like to use it in small amounts when I use other herbs like oregano, thyme, or parsley and in onion dishes. Add a pinch when you sauté or steam carrots or potatoes. Use savories in salads, soups, sauces, and stews and with poultry. And once you've tried putting a few sprigs of savory in your beans, whether they be French filet (young string beans) or pintos, you'll never fix them naked again.

Winter savory

SORREL
Rumex acetosa,
R. scutatus

Sorrel is a slightly lemon-flavored green herb that is sometimes cooked as a vegetable.

HOW TO GROW: There are two types of sorrel. Garden sorrel, *Rumex acetosa*, often mistakenly called French sorrel, and the true French sorrel, *R. scutatus*, sometimes called buckler sorrel. Garden sorrel is a fairly coarse-looking plant that grows to 2 feet (0.6 m) tall with 6-inch (15-cm)-long sword-shaped leaves. True French sorrel is a much smaller and refined plant, growing only to 6 inches (15 cm) tall with leaves an inch or so across. Both are very hardy plants, to USDA Zone 3, and flourish in all but the most extreme climates. Sorrels are generally planted from divisions, though they can also be planted from seeds in the spring. Locate plants in full sun or with some afternoon shade in rich, well-drained soil that is kept fairly moist. As sor-

rels can sometimes spread and become weeds, put them in the garden where they can be contained by paths or retaining walls, or grow them in containers. Fertilize in the spring and again in summer if the plants look pale. Divide the plants every three years to renew them. Protect the plants from slugs and snails, which relish the tender leaves.

HOW TO PREPARE: Sorrel leaves are used fresh in salads and sauces, particularly those for fish and asparagus. Try this herb in a savory bread pudding with baby artichokes; in meat pâtés, mayonnaise, and vichyssoise; and in a green aioli sauce. Sorrel's best-known use is in a rich French soup.

Garden sorrel
(**TOP**); true French
sorrel (**LEFT**)

SWEET WOODRUFF
Galium odoratum

This fragrant plant is known especially for its traditional use in May wine.

HOW TO GROW: Sweet woodruff's dark green foliage and tiny white flowers make an attractive ground cover in shade. The plant seldom grows higher than a foot (30 cm) and is hardy to USDA Zone 3. As its seeds are slow to germinate, it is usually propagated by division or transplants. Sweet woodruff prefers partial to full shade and rich, well-drained soil.

The German name for woodruff is *Waldmeister,* which literally means "Master of the forest." There it grows wild in the deep shade of pine forests. Traditionally the fragrant herb is collected just before it blooms, usually in the month of May, to make May wine. You may want to restrain it, as it is self-sowing and can become a weed. Mowing will help control sweet woodruff but will not harm it.

HOW TO PREPARE: Sweet woodruff has a faint vanilla fragrance that is stronger when the plant is wilted or dried. Pick the stems and dry them upside down in bunches. Sweet woodruff freezes well. The flowers can be used in salads. Fresh or dry leaves are used in tea or in May wine. In Germany one also finds this herb used as a flavoring for a gelatin dessert and a lovely syrup that is used to create the famous wheat beer, Berliner Weisse.

Sweet woodruff

TARRAGON
Artemisia dracunculus

Tarragon, sometimes called French tarragon, is a rich but delicately flavored herb with an anisey flavor. *Tagetes lucida*, variously called Mexican tarragon, Mexican mint marigold, and sweet marigold is a more assertive herb, but it has a similar flavor.

HOW TO GROW: French tarragon is a perennial hardy to USDA Zone 4 that grows to about 2 feet (0.6 m). The plant is started from divisions, never from seeds, and in the extremes of the coldest and hottest humid climates it must be started anew every spring. Happily, gardeners in the South can grow Mexican tarragon instead. This tender perennial is hardy only to USDA Zone 8, grows to about 3 feet (1 m), and has yellow flowers in late fall. It is semi-evergreen in the mildest winters but dies back to the ground if it freezes. Grow both tarragons in full sun (though they can tolerate some afternoon shade) and in rich, very well drained soil. Water moderately throughout the growing season.

When ordering plants, do not confuse French with Russian tarragon, which is much inferior in flavor and is sometimes sold as seeds. Both French and Mexican tarragons must be divided every few years to keep them growing vigorously. They have few pests, but French tarragon has occasional problems with root rot and mildew.

HOW TO PREPARE: Harvest leaves of both French and Mexican tarragons and use fresh anytime during the growing season. The French tarragon flavor does not preserve well, but if you want to try, put the leaves in vinegar or freeze them. Mexican tarragon dries fairly well. French tarragon adds richness and a slight anise flavor to sauces, particularly béarnaise sauce, and salad dressings; and the French have used it in omelets and on poultry, fish, and veal for centuries. Mexican tarragon has an affinity for corn, squash, tomatoes, and turkey. Use both tarragons sparingly, as the flavor is strong and can overpower a dish.

LEFT: Mexican tarragon **BELOW:** French tarragon

LEFT: 'Lime,' 'French,' and 'Wooly' thyme
BELOW: French thyme

THYME
Thymus spp

Thyme is versatile in the garden and the kitchen and is used in cuisines throughout the world. On a health note, thymes are very high in antioxidants.

HOW TO GROW: These spreading perennials vary from 4–12 inches (10–30 cm) in height and have either gray-green, dark green, golden, or silver foliage, depending on the variety. Some are more useful in the landscape, while others are more useful in the kitchen. French thyme, *T. vulgaris*, is the most commonly used culinary thyme. Other choice varieties are lemon thyme, *T. x citriodorus*, which has a rich lemon taste and pink flowers; caraway thyme, *T. herba-barona*, with a caraway taste, dark green leaves, and pink flowers; and 'Orange Balsam,' which has an orange flavor and is a favorite of West Indians. All the thymes need full sun and fast-draining soil. Most thymes are hardy to USDA Zone 5, but in cold-winter areas they need protective mulches. In spring cut back the foliage by about one third so the plant will stay lush. In mild climates many light prunings are needed during the growing season. Most gardeners start plants with transplants or by cuttings, though occasionally from seeds. Thymes are quite pest- and disease-resistant.

HOW TO PREPARE: Thyme can be harvested anytime throughout the growing season. It is wonderful fresh, though stripping the leaves off the stems can be tedious. Simplify the process by drying the stems until just brittle and then gently rubbing them between your palms to remove the leaves. Like parsley, thyme is a complementary herb and can be used in combination with most herbs for a more complex flavor. In fact, except for lemon thyme, I seldom use thyme alone. Small amounts of thyme complement many vegetables and most meat and fish dishes, soups, stews, salad dressing, and marinades, and try lemon thyme in a simple syrup to add to prosecco. Thyme is one ingredient of the traditional French *bouquet garni* and also of *herbes de Provence*. Try slipping a little lemon thyme under the skin of poultry before roasting or add it to mint tea. Thyme leaves can be dried as is or preserved in vinegar or oil.

My Favorite Herb Recipes

I have an amber jar of magic in my refrigerator. It's a marinade of olive oil crammed full of garlic and fresh basil leaves. When I add a spoonful of this oil to an omelet or a soup, I feel like Tinker Bell spreading magic dust. Presto! The dish explodes with flavor. Everyday foods become instant decadence. I spread this flavored oil on toast or in the pan before I cook potatoes. I use it in a salad or on green beans and zucchini. Sometimes I make herb butters, other times herb vinegar instead. And I use other herbs—maybe 'Cinnamon' basil, tarragon, or lemon thyme. To quote my grandmother, at any one time I have an elegant sufficiency of herbs.

Like most Americans, I grew up with few herbs in my food, and the ones I did know were dried. According to the late French chef Tom McCombie, "We Americans are so used to seeing our herbs labeled 'Schilling' or 'McCormick' that we expect them to be grown in the cans we buy them in. Most of us have no idea that basil and tarragon in their fresh form bear no resemblance to the dried products. In fact, many of our cookbooks call for 'tarragon' or 'parsley' and 'chervil' or 'parsley.' Well, they're all green, but that's really where the resemblance ends. In France, I worked in some of the greatest restaurants and I never once saw a can of herbs. I feel that's one of the main reasons French food is so good." Today, with a garden full of herbs, I know now that I grew up not color-blind but "herb-blind."

As a final note, the recipes in the following pages are primarily vegetarian.

Growing fresh herbs gives you the luxury of doing a little "show-off cooking." Sprigs of red basil, curly and flat-leaf parsley, sage, flowers of wild marjoram and chives, and the edible flowers of runner beans and violas are arranged to create showy canapés.

"Painting" with Garden Herbs

If you are new to herb gardening, a good way to begin learning about herbs is to think of a garden containing a dozen varieties of fresh herbs as a kind of palette of paints to work with in the kitchen. As with colors, the possibilities are endless. You can choose your medium and then the herb, or just the reverse. It's really hard to go wrong. Here are some ways to get started. But remember that in most cases fresh herbs are preferred over dried.

Let's begin with the medium of vegetables. For asparagus, try adding some chopped fresh dill leaves or tarragon to the mayonnaise you serve

it with. When you cook snap beans, add a little fresh chopped savory, basil, dill, or tarragon to the pan. If you are cooking dry beans in a recipe, add some thyme, oregano, basil, or savory, and for Mexican-style black beans, epazote.

A brief overview of the world's cuisines turns up a wealth of simple, time-tested ideas. In Germany, for instance, beets are sometimes served with caraway of dill, particularly if they are pickled. You might also want to try adding lemon balm. For eons people have enjoyed cabbage cooked with caraway, dill, mint or sage. The neutral flavors of the cabbages seem to soak up herb flavors readily. In France sweet, young carrots are often seasoned with dill, mint, chervil, thyme, or tarragon; and all over Europe cucumbers are flavored with dill, chervil, tarragon or basil. In the middle East cucumbers are combined with mints, and in India with cilantro. Eggplant, a favorite in southern parts of Europe, is often flavored with basil, thyme, oregano, fennel, or parsley. In India, it is the star of the spicy curry dish bharpha. The famous peas of the English are served with mint, and in other parts of the world cooks use thyme, chervil, and basil with their peas.

The sweetness of peppers combines naturally with the strong tastes of basil, oregano, or thyme; spinach is complemented by dill or basil in an omelet. Also try a dill-and-feta-cheese filling for filo-dough pastries or in crepes. Certain vegetables seem to have been created as vehicles for herb flavors—namely, potatoes, tomatoes, and summer squash. Try potatoes mashed or baked and sprinkled with parsley, tarragon, dill, chervil, or thyme; or roast them with rosemary or sage. And have tomatoes or summer squash with basil, oregano, parsley, thyme, fennel, anise seeds, mint, bay, cilantro, borage, rosemary, tarragon, or cumin.

> TIP: Most of us are trying to cut down on salt in our diet and fresh herbs provide a flavorful alternative. Instead of adding salt to, say, a vegetable soup or steamed beans, try a last-minute sprinkle of chopped fresh basil, dill, or tarragon.

Of course, other foodstuffs are also good vehicles for herbs. Take breads, for instance. I've already described my method of spreading olive oil seasoned with basil and garlic on toast. Also try adding fresh dill to your white bread or potato bread dough before baking. Or add sage to your biscuit dough when you make dumplings, rosemary on top of focaccia, and use basil in your cornbread.

Herbs have many uses, of course, with meats and fish of all types. Herbs add a new dimension to marinades—try one made of Italian seasonings on a London broil or hamburgers. Or for something more exotic, try chimichurri on London broil. Marinate pork in a sauce with sage, or chicken in a sauce with fennel. And sprinkle rosemary on lamb chops before putting them on the barbecue. A light sauce for fish is exquisite with just a hint of dill or chervil. A lamb stew is much more interesting when a handful of fresh chopped mint is added. Add chopped herbs of all types to hamburgers before cooking, or sprinkle them over a chicken before baking it. Also glazes made with herbs and jelly or mustard will spice up the blandest meat dishes.

Cheeses and egg dishes respond gloriously to fresh herbs. Layering soft cheese with chopped herbs makes a fancy but easy appetizer. Fill omelets and soufflés with fresh herbs and build a special brunch around baked eggs served with a sauce containing chopped dill or tarragon. Or try eggs Benedict with an herbed hollandaise.

Garnishes make up another medium. Use sprigs of fresh dill or fennel with fish, and place the beautiful leaves of golden sage around a tea sandwich tray. Sprigs of mint are nice in cold drinks and fruit salads. Teas too constitute a medium for fresh herbs. In particular, try the mints and the lemon- and anise-flavored herbs.

In the following section I've assembled many ways to feature the flavors of all types of herbs in combination, both fresh and dried, and in infusions of all types, and I have included many ways to preserve the essence of an herb for the winter.

ABOVE: English/French lavender sprigs give honey a subtle but rich flavor. Steep the sprigs in the honey then strain it. The fragrant honey can be drizzled over garden raspberries served with crème fraiche. **LEFT:** Assertive herbs such as fennel, sage rosemary, and oregano stand up well to bold flavors of garlic and chile peppers.

Fresh Herb Blends

The French are fond of herbs, and starting with a few French classics is a lovely way to begin. *Bouquet garni* and *fines herbes* are such versatile herb mixes, we've all probably used variations without calling them by their official titles. *Bouquet garni* is used to infuse a soup, stock, or sauce with complex flavors. Herbs are tied together with aromatic vegetables, added at the beginning of cooking, and removed at the end.

Bouquet Garni

1 small leek, or large leek sliced lengthwise,
    white part only
1 carrot
2 celery ribs, with greens
1 sprig fresh lovage
3 sprigs fresh parsley
3 sprigs fresh thyme
1 bay leaf

Tie all the ingredients together with clean white string. Leave a tail on the string so you can secure it to the pot and remove it easily.

Fines Herbes

Fines herbes is a mixture of chopped herbs. You will see dried mixes labeled "fines herbes," but the elusive flavors of the primary herbs—tarragon, parsley, and chervil—fade when dried. The traditional mixture calls for equal amounts of minced fresh parsley, tarragon, chervil, and chives or thyme. This mix is added at the last minute to soups, sauces, vinaigrettes, and savory egg dishes.

Gremolata

Here's another traditional herb blend—this one from Italy. It adds a "wallop" of flavor when sprinkled over osso buco, roast lamb, baked chicken, and fish; when added to soups before serving; or when stirred into marinades and sauces.

1 large lemon
1/2 cup chopped fresh Italian parsley
1 small garlic clove, minced
1/8 teaspoon salt
Dash of freshly ground black pepper

Grate the lemon peel. Place it in a small bowl, and mix in the parsley, garlic, salt, and pepper. It will keep for three days in the refrigerator.

Featured here (OPPOSITE TOP) are the work horses of the herb garden: flat-leaf and curly parsley, sage, rosemary, and French and lemon thyme. Use them in butters, pasta sauces, salad dressings, vegetable soups, poultry stuffings, meat stews, and in a marinade for roast meats. Even a garden with only a half dozen herb plants produces enough to share. Before a party, gather up little bouquets of fresh herbs, tie them with raffia, and take them to your host and hostess. Or dry the herbs in small quantities and give them as a bridal shower gift. For a festive presentation, put the dry herbs in a basket and add a great bottle of olive oil, a fancy vinegar, and your favorite salad dressing recipe.

A basic green salad can be given many faces by changing the selection of fresh herbs. Here are a number of fresh herb salad blends.

Asian Herb Blend

This herb mix can be used in a salad—try making the vinaigrette with rice wine vinegar and a little soy sauce, and add grilled scallops to the salad. This blend can also be added to a stir-fry at the end of cooking.

2 tablespoons chopped fresh cilantro
2 teaspoons minced fresh lemongrass
1 tablespoon finely snipped fresh Chinese chives

Classic Mesclun Herb Blend

Mesclun salad mixes are great from the garden and are now available in many markets. Traditionally, fresh herbs are included in the salad. Add the following herb blend to your mesclun next time and see what you think.

2 tablespoons chopped fresh chervil
1 tablespoon chopped fresh thyme
1 tablespoon chopped fresh tarragon

Fresh Flavor Herb Blend

Another herb variation adds dimension to vegetable salads. Try it on tomatoes and cucumbers, with avocados and root vegetables, or added to risotto.

1 tablespoon snipped fresh dill
2 teaspoons chopped fresh borage
1 tablespoon snipped fresh chives

Tangy Herb Blend

This blend is wonderful over a salad of mixed lettuces and tomatoes with a basic vinaigrette.

12–16 fresh sorrel leaves, chopped
2 tablespoons chopped fresh parsley
3 tablespoons fresh burnet leaves

Summer Essence Herb Blend

Use the following blend in tomato soup, on pizza, in a green or bean salad, or in just about any dish with lots of tomatoes.

2 tablespoons chopped fresh basil
2 teaspoons chopped fresh tarragon
1 tablespoon chopped fresh parsley

Dry Herb Blends

Drying herbs not only preserves the flavor for the off-season but sometimes can enhance the flavor as well. Many of the following blends have many variations under the same name, such as the classic *herbes de Provence*.

Roasted Root Vegetable Blend

Here's another roasting mix; you can use it inter-changeably with the Roast Potato Blend.

1 tablespoon dried rosemary
½ tablespoon dried savory
½ tablespoon dried thyme

Roasted Root Vegetables with Herbs

Serve these vegetables warm to accompany an omelet, meats, and fish or serve them at room temperature over a green salad or as a stand-alone buffet dish. This could be the star of a great vegan meal.

Serves 4

2 pounds (900 g) mixed root vegetables such as carrots, golden beets, parsnips, and turnips cut into 1-inch (2.5 cm) diameter pieces
2 pounds (900 g) new potatoes, about 1 inch wide, or larger ones cut into 1-inch (2.5 cm) pieces
3 tablespoons (45 ml) extra-virgin olive oil
Dash of salt
¼ teaspoon freshly ground black pepper
1 recipe Roasted Root Vegetable Blend
6 garlic cloves, chopped
3 tablespoons (45 ml) balsamic vinegar

Preheat oven to 350°F (175°C). It's important that the vegetables be the same size, so they'll cook at the same rate. Place them in a roasting pan approximately 10 x 13 inches (about 25 x 33 cm) and drizzle on the olive oil, season with salt and pepper, and stir to distribute the oil. Smooth out the vegetables into an even layer. Bake for 1 hour, stirring occasionally so they cook evenly. Remove the pan from the oven and sprinkle the herb blend and garlic over the vegetables and stir. Return the pan to the oven and bake for another 45 minutes or so, or until tender. Remove from the oven, sprinkle on the balsamic vinegar, and stir.

Herbes de Provence

In looking through French reference books, I found many different blends, all called *herbes de Provence*. The ones I gravitate toward are from Jacques Pépin and Antoine Bouterin. Other chefs add savory or sweet marjoram to the blend. According to Pépin, his blend is equal parts dried thyme, sage, rosemary, lavender, and fennel seeds. Use the blend with red meats and vegetables.

Herbes de Provence à la Bouterin

4 tablespoons dried thyme
2 tablespoons dried rosemary
1 tablespoon dried lavender
1 tablespoon fennel seeds
3 bay leaves, crushed

Tex-Mex Hot Barbecue Blend

A blend from a spicy part of the world, this mixture is great rubbed on beef, chicken, and pork before barbecuing. This recipe is for the "hot-heads"; if you don't like your food blazing, omit the chile Piquín.

2 tablespoons crumbled, dried Mexican oregano
1 tablespoon cumin seeds, toasted and ground
1 teaspoon chile Piquín flakes
1 teaspoon chili powder

Fresh Light Blend

Use this blend for poultry stuffing, in a lemon butter over fish, and added to soups.

2 tablespoons dried lemon thyme
1 tablespoon dried rosemary
1 tablespoon dried Greek oregano

Roast Potato Blend

2 tablespoons dried sweet marjoram
2 tablespoons dried thyme

For a delicious potato dish, parboil approximately 24 small potatoes (or ½ pound/ 250 g) until they're almost tender. Put them in a shallow baking pan to which 3 tablespoons (45 ml) of olive oil has been added, and stir to coat them. Sprinkle salt and pepper and the herb blend over them and stir again. Bake at 400°F (200°C), stirring occasionally until golden brown. (Bake about 20–30 minutes.)

Pestos

Pesto belongs in a basic vegetarian repertoire. It is generally defined as a paste of olive oil, garlic, nuts, Parmesan cheese (vegans can use a Parmesan cheese substitute), and fresh basil and is served as a sauce for pasta or is used as a flavoring for soup. But many modern chefs adhere to a more general definition, making a pesto with cilantro, peanuts, and peanut oil; mint with corn oil and walnuts; or even dry, without oil. The dry pesto has fewer applications, but again, it is a way to preserve that fresh flavor. Pestos are versatile as toppings for pizza, pastas, stews, and soups. Most can be incorporated into sauces for meats and mixed with yogurt, mayonnaise, or sour cream into dressings for salads. Finally, pesto freezes well and is a way to preserve the herb's flavor after the season is past. The following recipes are for a classic basil pesto and a dry rosemary pesto. They may be frozen in small canning jars and kept for four to six months. When freezing, leave out the cheese and add it just before serving. To prevent discoloration, place plastic wrap directly on the surface of the pesto before you freeze it.

Classic Pesto

Serve this pesto over fettuccine, or other pasta, either dry or fresh. Try combining cooked green snap beans or asparagus with the noodles for a lovely variation.

Makes approximately 1¼ cups (300 ml)

3 garlic cloves
2 cups fresh basil leaves
¼ cup (app. 35 g) pine nuts or walnuts
½ teaspoon salt
¼ teaspoon freshly ground black pepper
¾ cup (185 ml) extra-virgin olive oil
½ cup (50 g) freshly grated Parmesan cheese

In a blender or food processor, combine the garlic, basil leaves, nuts, salt, pepper, and half the oil. Puree, slowly adding the remaining oil. Transfer the mixture to a bowl and add the grated cheese, mixing thoroughly. Use immediately or cover with plastic wrap, since basil pesto turns brown if exposed to air. If you are going to serve this pesto over pasta, you may need to add a few tablespoons of cooking water to the pesto to make it the right consistency for the pasta.

Rosemary Pesto

Sometimes I make this pesto in a blender, but I find I must mince the garlic and finely chop the rosemary, or they don't blend properly. This pesto is added to a minestrone or tomato soup or sprinkled over a pizza before baking.

Makes about ½ cup

3 large garlic cloves, minced Handful of fresh
    Italian parsley leaves
Leaves from 2 (3-inch/8 cm) sprigs of fresh
    rosemary
6 tablespoons freshly grated Parmesan cheese
½ dried hot pepper

In a mortar, put the garlic, parsley, rosemary, Parmesan cheese, and hot pepper. Pound the ingredients with the pestle to a crumbly paste and serve.

Pesto is a speciality of the are around Genoa, Italy. All sorts of herbs can be used to make pesto. Rosemary is ideal for making a dry pesto to serve on minestrone soup or over a rich lamb stew.

Herb Vinegars

The flavors of many herbs are lost when the herbs are dried, but they can be preserved effectively in another form. Use white wine or rice wine vinegar for the milder herbs, and red wine vinegar for assertive herbs like oregano and rosemary. This method works well for dill, tarragon, thyme, lemon thyme, the basils ('Red Rubin' basil gives a beautiful magenta hue to vinegar, and 'Cinnamon' and 'Anise' basils impart pinkish tones), mint, or your favorite combinations. You may add other flavorings, such as garlic, onion, chives, hot peppers, or spices. If you want to make the vinegar in quantities for giving as gifts, you can buy vinegar at institutional supply houses in gallon jugs.

Use these herb-flavored vinegars in salad dressings, for marinades, in soups, or in just about any dish in which you would use unflavored vinegar. Try a mint vinegar in fruit salad or a tarragon vinegar in potato salad. Herb vinegars will store for up to a year.

Preserving in vinegar is one of the best ways to keep the flavor of basil over the winter. Use a wide-mouth jar to make it easy to add the herbs and garlic.

Red Rubin Basil Vinegar

Makes 1 pint (500 ml)

2 handfuls of roughly chopped fresh
   Red Rubin basil
4 garlic cloves, roughly chopped
1 pint (500 ml) white wine vinegar

Pack the basil loosely in a large, wide-mouthed pint jar (the stems and flowers can go in along with the leaves) and add the garlic. Fill the jar with vinegar. Cover and leave the jar in a dark place for one to two months. Strain the infusion through cheesecloth or a fine sieve, and then pour it through a funnel into bottles (clear glass shows off the colors best; use pretty bottles for holiday gifts), leaving any sediment at the bottom of the jar. Decorate the bottles with a sprig of the herb you used for flavoring, and then seal the tops.

Herb Oils

Oils are wonderful vehicles for herb flavors, and just about any oil will suffice. The best herbs for using in oils are sweet basil, lemon basil, dill, rosemary, tarragon, thyme, and lemon thyme. Use herb oils in salad dressings or as a substitute for butter on steamed vegetables such as carrots, zucchini, beans, broccoli, and cauliflower. Herb oil is also wonderful on toasted bread or as a chief ingredient in potato salad. Try dill oil drizzled over carrots or cucumbers, and basil or tarragon oil on tomatoes, zucchini, peppers, and potatoes. Lemon thyme oil is great over broccoli, carrots, cauliflower, and fish or chicken.

Many types of herb oils can be used to dress a salad.

Tarragon Oil

2 handfuls of roughly chopped fresh tarragon (approximately 2 cups)
1 dry hot pepper (optional)
1 pint (500 ml) pure virgin olive oil

In a sterile pint jar, place the tarragon and hot pepper (if desired). Cover it with olive oil, making sure that you have at least 1 inch of oil on top of the herbs. Refrigerate for 10 days. (The olive oil will solidify, but it reliquifies after a few minutes at room temperature.) After 10 days bring the oil to room temperature and strain. Discard the tarragon and hot pepper. Store the now completed oil in the refrigerator; it will keep for up to two weeks.

CAUTION: Storing at room temperature any oil with herbs or other foodstuffs in them can cause botulism. It is critical that herb oils be stored in the refrigerator.

NOTE: For safety reasons always remember to refrigerate your herb oils. In the refrigerator olive oil solidifies but soon becomes liquid again at room temperature.

Herb Teas

Chamomile, spearmint, and peppermint are all familiar herbs for tea, but pineapple sage, ginger mint, lemon-verbena, rosemary, fennel, and lemongrass make wonderful teas as well. Herb teas can be combined with white grape and apple juice and may be steeped with dried lemon or orange peel, ginger, anise seeds, and cloves to make more complex teas. Of course, individual herbs can be used, or you can combine herbs.

Herb teas can be made with either fresh or dried herbs and can be served either hot or cold. The general proportions are 1 teaspoon dried herbs to 1 cup (250 ml) water versus 1 tablespoon fresh herbs to 1 cup water. When making iced teas, double the amount of herbs, as the tea will be diluted with the melting ice.

To make a perfect cup of hot herb tea, first rinse the teapot with boiling water. Add the herbs, adding an extra teaspoonful for the pot, and pour in boiling water. Cover the pot and let it sit for 3–5 minutes. If it steeps too long, the tea gets bitter. Pour the hot tea out through a strainer into cups. Serve with sugar or honey and lemon.

May Wine Bowl

This recipe is from Rose Marie Nichols McGee of Nichols Garden Nursery in Albany, Oregon, and it is a variation on the traditional libation from Germany. Germans use this traditional punch to celebrate May Day. In Germany sweet woodruff grows wild in the woods and is collected before it flowers, to capture the best taste. Germans use only wilted or dry sweet woodruff and add champagne or sparkling water.

Serves about 20

5 bottles Moselle or Riesling wine
2 large handfuls sweet woodruff, cleaned
1 cup (250 ml) brandy
1 cup (225 g) sugar
A large ring mold of ice
1 cup (200 g) strawberries, Alpine or wild, if available

Pour 2 bottles of the wine into a large jar or crock, add 2 large handfuls of dry or wilted sweet woodruff, cover and refrigerate, and let stand for 3 days. Strain the infused wine into a large punch bowl and add the remaining 3 bottles of wine and the brandy, sugar, and ice. Add the strawberries to the bowl and decorate around the base of the bowl with sweet woodruff.

Chamomile Cooler

Chamomile is most beloved as a soothing herb tea. The following is Wendy Krupnick's iced variation that helps cool a hot day.

Serves 6

1 heaping tablespoon dried German chamomile
1 heaping tablespoon crushed, dried spearmint or peppermint leaves
1 quart (945 ml) apple juice
1 tablespoon (15 ml) lemon or lime juice (optional)

Garnish
Lemon slices and fresh mint leaves

Place the herbs in an ovenproof jar or pot. Pour 3 cups of boiling water over the herbs, cover the pot, and let it steep for 15–20 minutes. Strain the tea into a large pitcher. Add the apple juice and lemon or lime juice (if desired) and chill. Serve over ice and garnish.

Herb Butter

Serve this savory butter with a crisp French bread or melted over vegetables, fish, poultry, or a classic filet mignon. The butter can be rolled out between sheets of waxed paper and then cut into shapes with a very small cookie cutter. Here I have used tarragon, but chives, lemon thyme, rosemary, basil, or a combination of herbs can be used.

Tarragon Butter

Makes ½ cup (125 ml)

4 ounces (125 g/ 1 stick) unsalted butter at room temperature
2 tablespoons minced fresh tarragon
½ teaspoon lemon zest
1 tablespoon (15 ml) lemon juice

Cut the stick of butter in 6 or 8 pieces and then mash the butter with a fork to soften it. When it's fairly soft, slowly incorporate the tarragon, lemon zest, and lemon juice. Use a rubber spatula to transfer the mixture to a small bowl. Refrigerate until serving time.

Herb Cream

Nobody can boast of the health aspects of cream, but it sure does taste good. Add mint to the cream, whip it to serve with chocolate cake—or whip basil into your cream and serve it with strawberries. Steep it with savory for a sauce for potatoes and leeks, or steep it with basil and add it to custard. Flavored creams are the greatest.

Mint Whipped Cream

Makes 1½ cups (375 ml)

¼ cup chopped fresh spearmint or peppermint
1½ cups (375 ml) whipping cream
1½ tablespoons granulated sugar
¼ teaspoon vanilla extract

Place the mint and cream in a small saucepan over a low heat until small bubbles just begin to form around the sides of the pan. Do not let the cream boil. Cool. Pour the cream through a mesh strainer and discard the mint. Chill.

Just before serving, place the cream in a mixing bowl and whip it until the cream just starts to hold its shape. Add the sugar slowly as you mix. Add the vanilla and continue to whip until soft peaks form.

Interview:
The Saville Herb Garden

The first time I visited San Francisco Bay Area resident Carole Saville, she lived in Los Angeles, and I went to see her herb garden. As we chatted, she offered me some herb tea. I expected her to get out a jar of dried herbs, but instead she stepped out of her kitchen door and gathered

some fresh leaves of lemongrass and peppermint. Her teapot was glass, and when she put the leaves in it and poured boiling water over them, I could see the water turn bright green. That cup of tea I drank with honey was the best I had ever tasted.

When the time came to prepare dinner, out Carole went to her herb garden again, this time to gather snippets of tarragon and winter savory. She proceeded to slip the tarragon under the skins of Cornish game hens and chop the winter savory and put it in with the snap beans. When dinner was about ready, she went out once more to gather some crisp, fresh herbs and a few edible flowers for the salad. The meal had such richness and there were so many flavors woven through it from course to course that I realized, not for the first or last time, that I had a great deal to learn about herbs.

Since that day thirty years ago, Carole has become even more involved with herbs. When I first met her she was writing about cuisine and giving seminars on herbs. Much of that information is contained in her book *Exotic Herbs*, which is a must for anyone with access to many of the less familiar herbs, and is one of the few books that explores in detail ways to grow and prepare many exotic and unfamiliar herbs.

When Carole and I agreed that I would use her garden in my book, I asked her for some background, starting with how she had become interested in herbs. She told me that when she moved from New York City to a wonderful old house in New Jersey, she and her husband, Brent, decided to put in an herb garden because of her interest in cooking. After a few years she actually ended up with three herb gardens. The first was an informal one filled with culinary herbs, the next was an ornamental garden containing primarily plants with blue flowers, and the third was a traditional English knot garden.

Eventually, Carole moved to Los Angeles. On her cross-country flight she brought cuttings of some of her favorite herbs, and quickly installed them in a new herb garden. It was designed in a classic geometric pattern with a raised brick planter in the middle. And, of course, it was right off the kitchen. Today, Carole lives in Northern California in El Cerrito and limits herself to one herb garden. It contains all the culinary herbs she finds indispensable, including all the popular herbs, like thyme, basil, and sage and less common ones like sweet cicely, salad burnet, and nepetella. Bronze fennel pops up in her garden here and there, and she uses its fronds to flavor green peas or other vegetables. Carole plants chervil in pots both as decor and kitchen use to snip for green peas, among other vegetables. And both blue and white-flowered borage pops up here and there. The flowers are mostly used as decor in alcoholic drinks. Her rustic arugula reseeds itself in her garden from season to season, and she uses the delicious spicy leaves for salads. Recently her interest has turned to the many cultivars of traditional herbs such as 'Golden Rain' rosemary, 'African Blue' basil, and the many new herbs introduced by Southeast Asians. For instance she likes to combine lemon grass and Vietnamese balm in a subtle, fragrant lemonade and cilantro and Thai basil in chicken salad, generous amounts of chopped fresh thyme, marjoram, parsley, and dill in rice for herbed rice. She substitutes cilantro for basil in pesto, adds basil or chervil to mayonnaise, and my favorite, she chops rosemary or sage up fine and adds it to cornbread batter before baking it. As she says, "I just can't imagine cooking without my herb garden."

Carole Saville gathers herbs in her Los Angeles herb garden.

Herbed Vodka

I was surprised to learn that Carole also uses herbs in alcoholic creations such as rosemary infused in hard cider and spearmint or lemon balm in a refreshing aperitif, but her favorite use is to flavor vodkas.

"Flavored vodkas are ones that have either herbs, spices, or fruits added to them," she explained. "They first became popular in old Russia, where distillation and filtering methods were crude and something was needed to mask the tastes. The solution? Flavoring the liquor with fruits, berries, or herbs. In fact, Peter the Great habitually peppered his vodka, a practice thought to draw impurities to the bottom of the glass.

"Flavored vodkas have long had a following in Eastern Europe," Carole said. Old World favorites include Pertsovka, reputedly Stalin's favorite, which has the spicy taste of hot peppers; Okhotnichya, or hunter's vodka, flavored with herbs and berries; and Chesnochnaya, vodka infused with garlic, dill, and peppercorns.

While Russians drink flavored vodka throughout a meal, commonly referring to it as "the little ray of sunshine in the stomach," Carole likes to serve it with the first course—a nice way to begin a meal, she says. And while imported flavored vodkas are available in the United States from ethnic markets catering to Eastern Europeans, Carole recommends making your own. Commercial vodkas taste much stronger and certainly are not as fresh as home-made, and you can create your own combinations when you make them yourself. She usually combines the vodkas using the Fever-Tree line of mixers for the base.

When I asked Carole which flavors she likes best, she said, "I personally like to flavor vodka with mint, rosemary, or sweet woodruff, or with edible flowers such as roses, lavender, or dianthus—alone or in combinations. But I think everyone should be an alchemist and experiment in the kitchen! "I use only good-quality Russian or Swedish vodka or some of the American craft vodkas like Tito's," Carole emphasized, "because the primary flavor is still vodka. I put herbs in the vodka and keep it at room temperature for a day or two.

"Chefs and vodka aficionados have different opinions as to how long to infuse the herbs to achieve the best fragrance; the vodka will take on the flavor in just one day, but I like to leave it a little longer. Whatever your taste, the vodka is best if stored in a freezer because the liquid thickens slightly and the flavors become more pronounced.

"I save pretty bottles, about sixteen-ounce capacity, to transfer the vodka into when it's ready. I serve the vodka ice cold in ice-cold glasses with smoked salmon or other smoked fish or, if the pocketbook allows, caviar."

Carole likes to serve vodka in small, pretty glasses that she buys in antique shops. If the glasses are mismatched, she says, all the better. She prefers small glasses because they hold only small amounts; she thinks vodka should be sipped, and the smaller amount prevents people from getting drunk. As Carole said, "Drinking flavored vodkas, like using flavored vinegars and oils, is a way to enjoy the fresh taste of some of humanity's favorite herb flavors."

Flavored Vodkas

Makes 2 cups (500 ml)

2 cups (500 ml) good-quality vodka
1 tablespoon sweet woodruff leaves, or 2 tablespoons fresh lemongrass stalks cut diagonally from the white portion of the base into 1/4-inch (6–7 mm) slices, *or* 1 teaspoon coarsely chopped, fresh, English lavender

Combine the herbs and vodka in a very clean wide-mouth pint jar. Seal the jar and allow the mixture to steep for 24 hours at room temperature. Taste for flavoring. If a stronger flavor is desired, infuse the herbs for another 24 hours, or until the flavor suits you. Strain the mixture through a cheesecloth-lined funnel, and pour it into a sanitized, decorative pint bottle. Seal tightly with a cork or cap. Store the flavored vodka in the freezer.

Herb and flower vodkas (LEFT) made with roses, lemongrass, dianthus, English lavender, kumquats, sweet woodruff, and rosemary. Serve them ice cold. Here's Carole's recipe for Flavored Vodkas.

Gudi's Potato Pancakes with Chives

In some parts of Germany these pancakes are made with grated onions. Here Gudi Riter, my kitchen assistant, used chives for a milder flavor and for their lovely green snippets of color. In Germany these pancakes are traditionally served with applesauce for a brunch or lunch. They are best eaten immediately out of the pan, when they are still hot and crisp.

Serves 2 or 3 as a side dish, more as an appetizer

2 pounds (1 kg) Yukon Gold or Yellow Fins potatoes, peeled
1 medium-size onion, peeled
½ cup snipped fresh chives
2 eggs
3 tablespoons all-purpose flour
1 teaspoon salt
Freshly ground pepper and nutmeg
Vegetable oil

Garnish
Chive blossoms

Finely grate the potatoes. (The best texture is achieved by using the second-smallest grater on a four-sided hand grater. The opening is less than ⅛ inch [3–4 mm].) When grated, the potatoes will almost have the consistency of paste. Place the grated potatoes in a fine sieve or cheesecloth for about 15 minutes, to allow as much liquid as possible to drain. Squeeze the potatoes with your hands to extract more moisture if the mixture is still runny. (Some potatoes have more liquid than others.) When dry enough, the potato paste will more or less form a loose ball. Grate the onion using the same grater size.

In a mixing bowl, mix well the potato paste, grated onion, chives, and eggs. Add the flour, salt, pepper, and nutmeg to taste, and mix again.

In a large frying pan, add enough oil to cover the bottom of the pan to a depth of about ⅛ inch (3–4 mm). Heat the oil over medium heat. With a tablespoon, put a generous dollop of batter into the pan and flatten it with the back of the spoon to about the size of the palm of your hand. Fry the pancakes, three or four at a time until golden brown on both sides (approximately 3 minutes per side). Remove the potato pancakes from the pan and drain them on paper towels. Serve immediately with a garnish of chive blossoms. Makes 12–14 small pancakes.

Salmon, Cream Cheese, and Chive Torta

This stylish dish is great for a Sunday brunch served with bagels or as part of a buffet accompanied by crusty bread. The final flavor and texture of the dish depend on using good natural cream cheese, with no added gums, and choosing flavorful smoked salmon.

Serves 6

1 pound (500 g) natural cream cheese
½ cup plus 2 tablespoons snipped fresh chives
½ cup (app. 115 g) finely chopped smoked salmon

> **TIP:** The best way to cut chives is to snip them with scissors. If you have extra chopped chives put them in a small self-sealing freezer bag and freeze them. They can be added directly to marinades and cooked dishes in the winter and won't need defrosting.

In a small bowl, crumble half of the cream cheese, add ½ cup of the chives, and mix together with a fork. If necessary, add a few teaspoons of water to hold the mixture together and make it spreadable. Do not make it too soft, or the torta will not hold its shape.

To shape the torta, drape a small piece of cheesecloth to line a 2½- to 3-cup mold or straight-sided bowl. With a rubber spatula, form the bottom layer by spreading the chive and cream cheese mixture in the bottom of the mold, smoothing it out and filling any air holes.

In another bowl, crumble the remaining cream cheese and work in the salmon by repeating the procedure just outlined. Spread the salmon mixture on top of the chive mixture.

To unmold the torta, place a small serving plate facedown on top of the mold, making sure the cheesecloth is free of the plate and that the mold is centered on the plate. Hold the plate tightly against the top of the torta and turn the mold over. Lift off the mold and gently peel off the cheesecloth. To garnish, sprinkle the remaining 2 tablespoons of chives over the top.

Fancy Carrot and Onion Soup

This is a world-class soup! The sweet, bright flavors of carrots contrast beautifully with the dusky flavors of the lovage, coriander, and parsley in the onion soup garnish. The presentation is most dramatic if you serve the soup in individual shallow bowls.

Serves 4

4 cups (600 g) sliced carrots
2 tablespoons (30 ml) vegetable oil
2 cups (300 g) chopped onion
1 garlic clove, finely chopped
1½ cups (375 ml) chicken or
    vegetable broth
⅔ cup (160 ml) half-and-half,
    divided
1 tablespoons coriander or cumin
    seeds
2 stalks fresh lovage or fresh
    Italian parsley

Garnish
Small sprigs of dill or lovage, or
    carrot leaves

To make the carrot soup: Steam the carrots until tender. In a large pan, heat the oil and saute the onions until translucent, add the garlic, and saute 1 more minute. In a food processor or blender, puree the onion mixture. Transfer ½ cup (about 130 ml) of the onion puree to a small saucepan and set it aside. Leave the remaining onion mixture in the food processor.

Add the steamed carrots to the food processor and blend until smooth. Transfer the mixture to a saucepan, add the chicken broth, stir, and simmer 1 minute. Remove the carrot soup from the heat and set it aside.

To make the onion soup: In a dry, heavy frying pan, lightly toast the coriander or cumin seeds—keep stirring to prevent them from burning.

In a saucepan, heat ⅓ cup (app. 85 ml) of the half-and-half, add the toasted coriander or cumin seeds and the lovage or Italian parsley. Remove from the heat, and let the mixture steep for about 30 minutes to blend the flavors. Strain the seeds and herbs and discard them. Pour the flavored half-and-half into the saucepan with the reserved onion puree.

Before serving, reheat the carrot soup and stir in the remaining

⅓ cup (app. 85 ml) of the half-and-half, bringing it almost to a boil. Reheat the onion mixture. In both cases, do not let the mixtures boil or they will curdle.

To serve, half fill four individual shallow soup bowls with carrot soup. In the middle of each soup bowl, carefully ladle about ¼ cup (app. 65 ml) of the onion mixture.

Garnish with small carrot leaves, a sprig of lovage, or dill.

Stuffed Zucchini Blossoms with Goat Cheese

This elegant appetizer takes advantage of the midsummer zucchini explosion.

Serves 8 as an appetizer, 4 as a side dish

3 tablespoons (45 ml) extra-virgin olive oil, divided
1 medium onion, chopped
2 garlic cloves, minced
1 medium red bell pepper, roasted, seeded, and chopped
8 large paste tomatoes (2 pounds/ 1 k), peeled, seeded, and chopped
1 tablespoon (15 ml) tomato paste
1 teaspoon sugar
1 teaspoon balsamic vinegar
½ cup (125 ml) dry red wine
½ teaspoon chopped fresh thyme
¼ cup fresh basil, chopped
Salt and freshly ground black pepper to taste
8 small zucchini with their blossoms
6 ounces (170 g) creamy-style goat cheese
2 tablespoons fresh basil, chopped

Garnish
Fresh thyme leaves or chopped basil

In a large saucepan heat 2 tablespoons (30 ml) of the olive oil and saute the onions over medium heat until tender, about 7 minutes. Add the garlic and saute 4 minutes, or until they are soft but not brown. Add the bell pepper, tomatoes, tomato paste, sugar, and balsamic vinegar and simmer over low heat for about 45 minutes, or until the sauce is fairly thick, stirring occasionally. Add the wine, thyme, and basil and cook the sauce for 10 more minutes over medium heat. Press the sauce through a coarse sieve. You should have approximately 2 cups (500 ml) of sauce. Return the sauce to the saucepan, season with salt and pepper, and set it aside.

Preheat the oven to 350°F (175°C). Carefully examine the zucchini blossoms for insects and remove the stamens and pistils. In a small bowl blend the goat cheese with the basil. Fill each blossom with a scant tablespoon of the cheese. Try not to over-stuff the blossoms or the cheese will ooze out as it cooks. Brush the bottom of a baking dish with 1 teaspoon of olive oil. Place the zucchini into the dish and drizzle with the remaining oil. Bake for 15–20 minutes, or until they are al dente and starting to brown, and the cheese has melted.

Warm the sauce and divide it equally among the plates. Spread to create a small pool on each plate and place the stuffed zucchini in the middle of the sauce. Garnish with the herbs and serve.

Party Spinach Feta Strudel

This traditional flaky Greek dish has been the star at many a party. If your filo dough is frozen, defrost it overnight in the refrigerator. Remove the filo dough from the refrigerator at least 3 hours before preparing the strudel. Try this as the star of a vegetarian buffet.

Makes about 60 (3-inch/8 cm) pastries

3 (1-pound/ 500 g) packages of filo (strudel) dough
2 pounds (1 k) fresh spinach
1/3 cup (80 g) salted butter
1 1/2 cups (225 g) finely chopped onions
5 eggs, slightly beaten
1 pound (500 g) feta cheese
1 cup chopped fresh dill
1/4 cup chopped fresh Italian parsley
1/4 teaspoon freshly ground black pepper
2–3 cups (500–750 g/4–6 sticks) unsalted butter

To prepare the filling:
Wash the spinach well in two or three changes of water. Put an inch of water in the bottom of a steamer and bring it to a boil. Steam half the spinach until just wilted, remove, and put in a large bowl. Repeat this procedure with the rest of the spinach. Cool the spinach and by hand squeeze out most of the liquid, then coarsely chop.

Melt the salted butter in a skillet over low heat. Add the onions and slowly cook until translucent, about 10 minutes. Add the onions to the spinach. Cool. Add the eggs, feta cheese, dill, parsley, and pepper and mix well. Chill for 30 minutes. If liquid collects, drain the mixture.

To assemble the pastries:
Have on hand three cookie sheets, a damp, clean dish towel, and a pastry brush. In the microwave oven, melt the unsalted butter in a small bowl. When working with filo dough, never let it dry out. Cover it with a barely damp dish towel.

Lay one sheet of filo dough on a clean surface and lightly paint a thin layer of melted butter on it. Lay another sheet on top, repeating this process until you have created four layers. Paint the top layer with butter. Cut strips approximately 3 inches (8 cm) wide, cutting across the width (shortest dimension) of the layered filo. Place approximately 1 1/2 teaspoons of spinach filling 1 inch in from the end of one strip. Fold a corner of the strip diagonally over the filling to form a triangle, then fold the triangle over itself all the way to the end, just as you would fold a flag. Brush it with butter and place it on a cookie sheet. (Your first few pastries will probably be uneven, but you'll soon perfect the technique.) Repeat with the remaining strips. Continue the layering procedure with the rest of the filo dough. Any leftover filling can be used to fill an omelet. (Pastries can be frozen at this point. Put them in the freezer on a cookie sheet lined with waxed paper. When they're completely frozen, transfer them to plastic freezer bags.)

Preheat the oven to 350°F (175°C). Bake for 35 minutes, or until golden brown. Serve warm.

Spinach and Fresh Oregano Pizza

Pizza and fresh oregano are perfect partners. This is a basic pizza; chopped bell peppers, sliced tomatoes, or grilled eggplant may be substituted for some of the vegetables below. Vegetarians can omit the sausage.

Serves 4

2 teaspoons (10 ml) olive oil
1 small onion, minced
1 garlic clove, minced
¼ pound (125 g) Italian-style pork or turkey
    sausage, crumbled or sliced
4 or 5 mushrooms, sliced
3 cups (675 g) fresh spinach
Freshly ground black pepper
1 large unbaked pizza shell
¼ cup (25 g) feta cheese, diced
1–1½ teaspoons finely chopped fresh oregano
1 cup (100 g) grated mozzarella cheese

Preheat oven to 450°F (230°C). In a large pan, heat the olive oil and saute the onions, garlic, sausage, and mushrooms for about 10 minutes, or until the sausage is cooked. Add the spinach and saute, stirring constantly, for about 1 minute, or until the spinach has wilted. Add pepper to taste. Spread the mixture on the pizza shell. Sprinkle on the feta cheese and the oregano, and top with the grated mozzarella. Bake for 10–15 minutes, or until the cheese has melted and the shell starts to brown.

Barbecued Vegetables on Rosemary Skewers

Sometimes gardener-cooks can't help themselves and have to do some "show-off" cooking. Certainly using the stout stems of upright, woody rosemaries like 'Tuscan Blue' or 'Miss Jessup's Upright' as barbecue skewers qualifies as one-upmanship cooking. You can use any recipe that requires grilling on skewers, just remember to soak the rosemary skewers and keep them away from the hottest coals. Great hors d'oeuvres for a vegetarian meal!

Serves 4

- 4 strong, straight, woody stems of rosemary, ¼–⅓ inch (6–9 mm) in diameter and 10–14 inches (25–35 cm) long
- 8–12 large red or orange cherry tomatoes, or 2 medium paste tomatoes cut in quarters
- 8–12 boiling onions (1–1½ inches /25–40 mm in diameter), peeled and parboiled for 2 minutes
- 1 medium-size Japanese eggplant, cut in 6 slices
- 1 medium-size red or yellow bell pepper, cut into approximately 12 (1-inch/2.5 cm) pieces
- 1 medium-size green bell pepper, cut into approximately 12 (1-inch/2.5 cm) pieces

Marinade
- ⅓ cup (85 ml) extra-virgin olive oil
- 1 large garlic clove, minced
- 2 tablespoons finely chopped fresh rosemary

Thirty minutes before you are ready to grill the vegetables, prepare the rosemary skewers and the fire. To prepare the skewers, strip the leaves off each stem by holding on to the top with one hand and grasping the stem tightly with the thumb and forefinger of your other hand and running them down the stems. Soak the stems in water for half an hour before using them. To prepare the fire, place a single layer of charcoal in your kettle grill and light it.

Divide the vegetables into four equal portions, making sure that there are vegetables of each type for each skewer. Take the rosemary skewers and thread each vegetable onto them, one at a time, alternating the different vegetables. (If the ends of the rosemary are not sharp enough to penetrate some of the vegetables, make a small hole in the vegetables with a knife.) Fill each skewer but leave an inch at the end for a handle.

To make the marinade, in a small bowl, stir together the olive oil, garlic, and rosemary. With a small brush, paint the marinade on both sides of the vegetables. Paint them again before you are ready to cook them.

When the flames have died down and the charcoal is covered with a fine gray ash, it's time to cook your skewered vegetables. Grease the grill well and place it about 6 inches (15 cm) above the coals—or at the distance where you can hold your hand for about a second. Place the skewers on the grill and turn them about every 2 minutes, until they are tender and start to brown—about 8 minutes.

Goat Cheese Cheesecake with Herbs

This is a contribution from Jesse Ziff Cool, chef and owner of the Flea Street Cafe in Menlo Park, California. Try serving it as an appetizer with crisp apples and warm, crusty bread or home-made garlic toast. The cheese-cake must be refrigerated over-night, so plan ahead. However, it can keep for weeks. This is a great vegetarian dessert!

Serves 20 as an appetizer

2 pounds (1 k) fresh goat cheese
1 pound (500 g) cream cheese
3 eggs
2 tablespoons minced fresh
    rosemary, oregano, or thyme, or
    a combination of all three
¾ cup (120 g) finely chopped sweet
    red peppers
About 1 cup (135 g) pine nuts

Preheat the oven to 375°F (190°C). Soften the goat and cream cheeses, and whip together all the ingredients except the pine nuts. Butter an 8-inch springform pan and pour in the goat cheese mixture. Spread the pine nuts evenly over the top and bake for 25–30 minutes. Cool to room temperature, cover, and chill the cheesecake in the refrigerator overnight. Slide a wet knife around the outside of the cheese-cake to loosen it. Remove the spring and lift off the ring. Slide the cheese-cake onto a plate if you choose, or simply serve it from the pan bottom. Serve at room temperature.

Watermelon Salad with Black Grapes and Tarragon

Most cooks use herbs in savory rather than sweet dishes such as this sophisticated fruit salad, which can be served as an appetizer or a dessert. I like to use yellow watermelon and black seedless grapes in this dish, and use only fresh tarragon, as dried has much less flavor. This dessert would be the perfect end to a vegan meal.

Serves 4

2–2⅓ cups (300–450 g) seeded and
    cubed yellow or red watermelon
2 cups (350 g) seedless grapes,
    halved
½ cup (125 ml) white grape juice
1 teaspoon honey
1 teaspoon finely chopped fresh
    tarragon
Lemon sorbet

Garnish
Small slices of watermelon and
    grapes, sprigs of tarragon

Place the watermelon and grapes into a medium-size bowl.

In a small bowl, combine the grape juice, honey, and tarragon. Pour it over the fruit and gently mix together. Divide the mixture equally among four serving bowls. Top each with a small scoop of lemon sorbet. Place the bowls on small plates and garnish with a watermelon slice, grapes, and tarragon on each plate.

Golden Beets with Dill Vinaigrette

Golden beets are startlingly beautiful; paired with dill, they taste sweet, rich, and earthy.

Serves 4

6 medium-size golden beets
⅓ cup (80 ml) olive oil
3 tablespoons (45 ml) white
   wine vinegar
1 teaspoon minced fresh dill
Salt and freshly ground black
   pepper
1 large head of butter lettuce,
   leaves washed and separated

Garnish
Purple pansies or nasturtiums

Wash the beets and steam them for approximately 40 minutes, or until just tender. Peel and slice them. While they are still warm, make the vinaigrette.

In a bowl, stir the oil, vinegar, and dill. Pour the vinaigrette over the beets and gently stir; let the beets sit for an hour at room temperature to absorb some of the flavors, stirring them occasionally. Refrigerate. On a large platter, arrange lettuce leaves, top them with the beets, and garnish with flowers.

Native Squash Stew

This main dish stew is a great surprise to anyone having it for the first time. As my brother-in-law in Maine says, "It's awesome," and he serves it with corn bread and a salad. My son-in-law in Los Angeles thinks it's great with warm corn tortillas. Choose a rich-flavored squash such as butternut, 'Gold Nugget,' or kaboucha; it's a perfect marriage. This stew freezes beautifully, thus the large proportions for the following recipe. You can easily change the spiciness of the dish by deleting or adding more roasted chiles or adding more hot sauce. This dish is wonderful vegan main meal.

Serves 8

3 tablespoons (45 ml) oil
2 medium-size to large
   onions, chopped
9–10 cups (app. 2.75–3.5 k)
   winter squash, peeled and
   cut into 2-inch (5-cm) cubes
4 garlic cloves, finely chopped
1 red bell pepper, roasted,
   peeled, and chopped
4–2 fresh mild green

Anaheim Chiles, roasted, peeled,
   and chopped, or 1 or 2 small cans
   of mild Chiles, chopped
2 or 3 ears of corn, scraped, or
   1 can (400 g) of niblet-style corn
2–3 teaspoons ground cumin
Salt and freshly ground black pepper
Hot pepper sauce

Garnish
3–4 tablespoons finely chopped fresh
   cilantro

In a large stockpot, heat the oil and add the onions. Saute over medium heat until translucent. Add the squash, garlic, bell pepper, chiles, corn, cumin, and 3 cups (750 ml) of water, cover, and simmer over low heat for 30–45 minutes, or until the squash is tender.

Add salt, pepper, and your favorite hot sauce to taste. Transfer the stew to a large serving bowl and sprinkle with cilantro.

Leeks and New Potatoes with Savory Cream

The herb savory brings out the richness of the vegetables. Nowhere is it more evident than in this voluptuous dish in which it flavors leeks, cream, and potatoes. Another great vegetarian dish.

Serves 4 as a side dish

1 pint (500 ml) whipping cream
4 (3-inch/8 cm) sprigs of fresh winter savory, divided
14–16 new potatoes (2–2½ inches /5–6 cm) in diameter, washed but not peeled
1 teaspoon salt
10–12 young leeks, ½–1 inch (1.5–2.5 cm) in diameter, or 4 large leeks
1 tablespoon (14 g) butter
¼ teaspoon nutmeg
Salt and freshly ground black pepper

Garnish
Fresh sprigs of winter savory.

Put the cream and 3 sprigs of the savory in a saucepan and bring it to a boil. Remove from the heat and let the cream steep for about 1 hour.

In another saucepan, boil the potatoes in water with salt and the remaining sprig of savory until just tender, approximately 20 minutes.

Clean the leeks by partially cutting them lengthwise and flushing them with water. Cut the white parts diagonally in pieces approximately 2 inches (5 cm) long. (For large leeks, cut into 1-inch/2.5-cm pieces.) If the lower portions of the green leaves are tender, slice them as well. (Use tough green tops to make stock.) Saute the leeks in butter for 5 minutes, or until tender, and set aside.

Remove the savory sprigs from the cream and discard. Bring the cream to a boil and reduce until about half remains, approximately 6–10 minutes. Season with nutmeg, salt, and pepper.

To serve, reheat leeks if necessary. Arrange the leeks on part of a serving plate. Drain the potatoes and place them on the other side of the plate. Pour the reduced cream over the leeks and potatoes and garnish with savory sprigs.

Roast Lamb with Rosemary

Lamb with rosemary is a classic combination. Serve the lamb with roasted or mashed potatoes and spring vegetables—a fresh peas would be classic. If you opt to use ground dried rosemary, avoid the bottled version from the market, as it seldom has much flavor. Instead, put dry leaves of rosemary in an electric coffee grinder, and grind your own. (Using this inexpensive appliance is well worth the flavor boost that fresh-ground seasonings give to food.) The lamb should marinate for at least 4 hours.

Serves 5 to 6

1 tablespoon finely minced fresh
  rosemary or 1 teaspoon ground
  dried rosemary ½ cup (125 ml)
  Dijon-style mustard 1 garlic clove,
  mashed to a paste
1½ tablespoons extra-virgin olive oil
1 leg of lamb (5½–6 pounds/ 2.5–3 k)

Place the rosemary, mustard, and garlic in a small bowl. Whisk in the oil a few drops at a time until all the oil has been incorporated.

To prepare the lamb, remove most of the outer layer of fat, leaving a thin layer of filament over the meat. Brush the rosemary mixture over the entire leg of lamb. Refrigerate for at least 4 hours.

Preheat the oven to 350°F (175°C). Place the lamb in a shallow roasting pan and bake for 1½–2 hours, or until a meat thermometer reads 145°F (63°C) for medium rare. Carve the lamb into thin slices before serving.

Grilled Swordfish with Rosemary

This recipe from Carole Saville blends the richness of swordfish with the assertiveness of rosemary. It works equally well when broiling the swordfish instead. Note that the swordfish needs to marinate for an hour.

Serves 4

¼ cup fresh rosemary leaves
  and soft stems
1 cup (250 ml) olive oil
2 tablespoons (30 ml) lemon
  juice
¼ teaspoon salt
Cayenne pepper
4 swordfish steaks, 1 inch
  thick (about 5 ounces/
  140 g) each

Garnish
4 teaspoons finely chopped
  fresh rosemary, rosemary
  flowers (if in bloom), and
  lemon wedges

Finely chop the rosemary. Put it in a small bowl and with the bottom of a drinking glass rub the rosemary to bruise it. In a large, deep plate, combine the olive oil, lemon juice, salt, cayenne pepper, and rosemary, stirring to combine. Rinse the swordfish and pat it dry. Turn each steak over in the marinade to coat it well. Cover and refrigerate the swordfish for 1 hour, turning it once after 30 minutes.

Grill the swordfish over a medium flame, turning it after 5 minutes. Continue to grill until the flesh is opaque when cut in the thickest part, about 5 more minutes. Remove the steaks and place on four warmed plates. Sprinkle a bit of chopped rosemary over each. Garnish with rosemary flowers and lemon wedges. Serve immediately.

Carrots and Apricots with Fresh Chervil

Carole Saville and I wrote an herb series for *Country Living Gardener* for many years and when I asked her what chervil recipes were her favorites, she gave me this one. You'll see that apricots and chervil add a sprightly note to steamed carrots.

Serves 4

¼ cup (app. 70 g) slivered dried apricots
1 pound (500 g) carrots
2 tablespoons (30 ml) walnut oil
2 tablespoons (30 ml) fresh squeezed orange juice
Salt and freshly ground black pepper
½ teaspoon anise seeds
2 tablespoons minced fresh chervil

In a small bowl, cover the apricots with hot water and set them aside to plump for 30 minutes. Peel the carrots and cut them into thin slices. Steam the carrots for 5–10 minutes, or until they're tender but not soft. Remove them from the steamer basket and discard the water, then return them to the warm pot. Drain the apricots and add them to the carrots. Stir in the walnut oil, orange juice, salt, and pepper to taste, and cover the pot. Heat the anise seeds in a small, dry cast-iron skillet, stirring constantly just until they perfume the air, about 1 minute. Add the anise seeds and chervil to the carrots. Stir to combine. Serve immediately.

Savory Mashed Potatoes with Garden Herbs

Traditional mashed potatoes are wonderful, but adding chopped fresh herbs means infinite variations.

Serves 4

2–2½ pounds (1–1.25 k) Yukon Gold or Russet-type potatoes (app. 4 large), peeled and cut into quarters
2 garlic cloves
½ cup (125 ml) milk
⅓ cup (80 ml) heavy cream
4 tablespoons (60 g) butter
1½ teaspoons finely snipped fresh chives
1 tablespoon finely chopped fresh parsley
1½ teaspoons finely chopped fresh tarragon
Dash of nutmeg
Salt and freshly ground black pepper

In a large saucepan, cover the potatoes and garlic with water and boil for 10–15 minutes, or until potatoes are tender. Be careful to not overcook them. Drain off the water.

Meanwhile, in a small saucepan, heat the milk and cream. When the mixture is hot but not boiling, add the butter and continue heating until the butter has melted.

Force the potatoes and garlic through a ricer or food-mill, or mash them in a bowl with a potato masher until they are smooth. (Be careful not to overmix them, or the potatoes will get gummy.) Place the potatoes in a large saucepan and over medium heat, slowly stir in the milk mixture with a spoon until it has a creamy texture. Fold in the herbs. Add salt and pepper to taste.

Fennel Rice with Pistachios

This "fragrantly" flavorful dish makes a wonderful accompaniment for fish or roasted chicken, or you can add grated cheese before you cover the rice with the breadcrumb mixture for a vegetarian main course. I prefer to use Carolina or Basmati rice as they have a light, rich texture.

Serves 6

2 cups (450 g) uncooked white long-grain rice,
4½ cups (1 l) vegetable broth, divided
1 bay leaf
2 Florence fennel bulbs (3–4 inches/ 8–10 cm wide) with greens (app. 2 pounds/ 1 k)
2 tablespoons (30 ml) olive oil
1 large onion, coarsely chopped
2 garlic cloves, minced
1 teaspoon fennel seeds
1 teaspoon coriander seeds
2 tablespoons chopped fresh parsley
Salt and freshly ground black pepper to taste
1 cup (100 grated Gruyere cheese, optional)
1½ cups (135 g) fresh bread crumbs
½ cup (65 g) chopped shelled pistachio nuts or shelled almonds
⅛ teaspoon freshly ground black pepper, plus extra
1 tablespoon (14 g) butter, melted

Place the rice in a large saucepan or rice cooker. Add 3½ cups of the vegetable broth and the bay leaf. Bring it to a boil, then cover and cook over low heat for about 20 minutes, or until the rice is tender and the liquid has been absorbed. Remove the bay leaf.

Meanwhile, remove the fennel leaves from the stems, setting aside a few leaves for a garnish. Finely chop the leaves. Cut the fennel bulbs crosswise into fine dice.

In a large frying pan, heat the olive oil over medium heat. Add the onions, garlic, and diced fennel bulbs and saute, stirring occasionally, for about 10 minutes, or until translucent.

With a blender or mortar and pestle, coarsely grind the fennel seeds and coriander seeds.

In a large bowl, combine the onion mixture, cooked rice, chopped fennel greens, parsley, and the ground coriander and fennel seeds. Add salt and pepper to taste.

(At this point you could stir in the nuts and serve immediately as a simple side dish.)

Preheat the oven to 350°F (175°C). Grease a 3-quart (medium) shallow ovenproof casserole dish. Add remaining vegetable broth to the rice and mix. Spread the rice mixture evenly in the dish. Sprinkle grated Gruyere cheese over the rice, if desired. In a small bowl, combine the bread crumbs, nuts, and the ⅛ teaspoon of black pepper. Sprinkle the bread crumbs over the rice. Drizzle melted butter on top. Bake for about 15 minutes, or until the top is a light golden brown. Serve garnished with fennel leaves.

Planting and Maintenance

Covered in this section are the basics of planning a vegetable garden, preparing the soil, starting seeds, transplanting, fertilizing, composting, using floating row covers, rotating crops, mulching, watering and installing irrigation, and maintaining vegetables.

Planning Your Herb Garden

The first step in planning your garden is choosing a suitable site. Most chefs recommend locating the herb garden as close to the kitchen as possible, and I heartily agree. Beyond that, the majority of herbs need at least six hours of sun (eight is better) and great drainage. There are only a few culinary herbs that grow well in shade: angelica, chervil, mint, parsley, sorrel, and sweet woodruff. Annual herbs—namely, basil, chervil, dill, and cilantro—the biennial parsley, and a few of the perennial herbs need fairly rich soil with lots of added organic matter. Think of these herbs as growing under the same conditions as annual vegetables. They can be planted in a bed by themselves—as part of the classic vegetable garden, say—or interplanted in a flower bed with annual flowers, most of which need the same conditions. All these herbs can also be grown in containers or in large planter boxes. Most perennial herbs, including many from the Mediterranean, such as thyme, rosemary, sage, oregano, lavender, and fennel, grow best

with good amounts of organic matter but less nitrogen. They need fast-draining, neutral soil, fairly low fertility, and only enough water to grow well. These plants can be grown in an area by themselves or used as flowering shrubs in a permanent border, on hillsides, and in all sorts of containers.

Once you've decided on where you are going to plant, it's time to choose your herbs. Your major consideration will be, of course, what flavors you enjoy using in the kitchen. With this in mind, look for species and varieties that will grow well in your climate. As a rule, gardeners in northern climates and high elevations need herb species that tolerate cool and/or short summer conditions and often cold winters. Gardeners in hot, humid areas require plants that tolerate diseases well and don't wither in the heat. In addition, some herbs like tarragon and angelica need winter cold to grow well. Hot, arid conditions dictate choosing plants that are drought-tolerant and avoiding plants with large, fleshy leaves (like lovage and sorrel), which tend to struggle in this climate. Opt for Mediterranean herbs with small, gray foliage. The USDA Plant Hardiness Zone map (right) has grouped eleven zones according to winter lows, which is helpful in choosing perennial herbs to ensure they survive in the winter. The *Sunset National Garden Book* map gives even more detailed climate information; it divides the continent into forty-five growing zones. This information-packed resource book, published by Sunset Books, details thousands of plants, including hundreds of herbs, and gives their growing zone. The The Plant-Heat Zone Map, published by the American Horticultural Society, is of equal value to much of the country, as once a gardener determines whether a plant is going to survive the winter, he or she needs to know how much heat the plant requires or can withstand. The heat map details twelve zones that indicate the average number of days each year when a given area experiences temperatures of 86°F (30°C) or higher—the temperature at which many plants begin to suffer physiological damage. In the herb encyclopedia I detail a number of herb species, indicating those with a low tolerance to high temperatures and, where possible, giving alternative herbs with the same flavors.

In addition to analyzing your climate, knowing what type of soil a particular herb needs is equally important. Consider how well your soil drains: is it rich with organic matter and fertility? Poor soil with bad drainage? So sandy that few plants grow well? Find out too what your soil pH is; nurseries have kits to test your soil's pH, and University Extension Services can lead you to soil experts. As a rule,

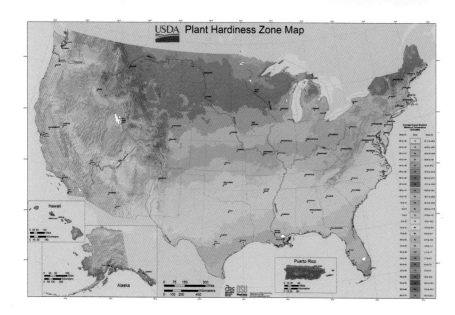

The Plant Hardiness Zone Map. Photo courtesy of the Agricultural Research Service, USDA. planthardiness.ars.usda.gov (see also www.ahsgardening.org/gardeningresources)

rainy climates have acidic soils that need the pH raised, and arid climates have fairly neutral or alkaline soils that need extra organic matter to lower the pH. Is there hardpan under your garden that prevents roots from penetrating the soil, or water from draining? This is a fairly common problem in areas of heavy clay. You need answers to these basic questions before you proceed because, while they are among the easiest plants to grow, herbs do have limits. With few exceptions, herbs do best with good drainage. Their roots need air, and if the soil stays waterlogged for long, roots suffocate or are prone to root rot. If you are unsure of how well a particular area in your garden drains, dig a hole about 10 inches (25 cm) deep and 10 inches (25 cm) across and fill it with water. The next day fill it again—if it still has water in it eight to ten hours later, you need to find another place in the garden that will drain much faster, amend your soil with much organic matter and mound it up at least 6–8 inches (15–20 cm) above the ground level, or grow your herbs in containers.

Once you have chosen a nice sunny area, selected a garden design, and determined that your soil drains properly, you are ready to prepare the soil.

PREPARING THE SOIL

To prepare the soil for a new garden of herbs, first remove large rocks and weeds. Dig out any perennial weeds and grasses, making sure to get out all the roots, or they will come back and, unfortunately, up through your new herb plants. If you are taking up part of a lawn, the sod will need to be removed. If it is a small area, this can be done with a flat spade. Removing large sections, though, warrants renting a sod cutter. Next, when the soil is not too wet, spade over the area. If you are going to be planting many annual herbs and may be adding salad greens, veg-

etables, and annual flowers, you need to supplement your soil with a lot of organic matter and an organic nitrogen fertilizer, as most soil is deficient in these materials. Very sandy soil also needs a lot of added organic matter to help hold moisture and fertility. A garden of mostly perennial herbs, though, in average soil needs no added fertilizer, except some bonemeal worked into the top 8 inches (20 cm) of soil before planting, at the rate of 4 cups per 100 square feet (30 m). After the area has been spaded up, cover it with 4–5 inches (10–12 cm) of compost and an inch or two of well-aged manure. Add even more compost if you live in a hot, humid climate where heat burns the compost at an accelerated rate, or if you have very alkaline, very sandy, or very heavy clay soil. Since most herbs grow best in a neutral soil, add lime at this point if your soil is acidic. Follow the directions on the package. If you are planting a number of annual herbs or adding vegetables and annual flowers, sprinkle fish fertilizer or chicken manure over the beds where they are to be planted. Incorporate the ingredients thoroughly by turning the soil over with a spade. If your garden is large or the soil is very hard to work, you might use a rototiller. (When you put in a garden for the first time, sometimes one is needed. However, research has shown that continued use of tillers is hard on soil structure and quickly burns up valuable organic matter if used regularly.) If you can do this soil preparation a few weeks before you plant, so much the better.

Finally, grade and rake the area. You are now ready to form the beds and paths. Because of all the added materials, the beds will now be elevated above the paths—which further helps drainage. Slope the beds away from the paths so loose soil will not be washed or knocked onto the paths. Some gardeners add a brick or stone edging to out-

TO DIVIDE PERENNIAL HERBS
Use a sharp spade to cut down through the middle of the clump (**TOP**). Lift the clump out of the ground (**MIDDLE**). Once the herb is out of the ground cut the clump in three or four pieces with a spade (**BOTTOM**). Each piece is now a new plant and can be given its own planting hole. Cut the divided plants back by at least half and water them in.

line the beds. Some sort of gravel, brick, stone, or mulch is needed on the paths to prevent weeds, to give a strong design to your garden, and, most important, to prevent your feet from getting wet and muddy. Once paths are in place, lay out plants where they are to be planted. Choose short species for the front of the beds and tall ones for the rear. Step back and see how you like the color contrast of foliage and flower you have chosen, then finetune your design. Also refresh your memory as to how far the plants will spread, so they won't be crowded once they mature. Few gardeners get it right the first time, however. I always make a few mistakes and end up moving herbs around as the design comes together. That's half the fun.

One last possible step to consider for herb gardens in cool-summer areas or in hot, humid climates is that of applying a pebble mulch. In cool-summer gardens they provide extra heat to the plant by absorbing it in the day and releasing it back at night. I once visited Gwen Barclay and her mother the late Madaline Hill in hot, humid Texas, and they find that a 2-inch (5 cm) gravel mulch helps provide a cool root zone and gives fast drainage, both of which help prevent fungus problems for drought-tolerant herbs. Before installing them, clear the ground of weeds, especially perennial ones, as removing the gravel mulch to replant is a daunting project. To make sure weeds don't come up through any type of mulch, some gardeners report success by placing six to eight layers of damp black-and-white newspaper sheets down before adding the gravel.

TRANSPLANTING

I generally start my herbs from plants, not seeds. I obtain my plants from divisions—clumps taken off of mature herbs growing in my garden or a friend's—or I buy transplants from the local nursery or from online nurseries; in some cases I start them from cuttings. (All but the most unusual perennial herbs, and many annual herbs, are available from retail and online herb nurseries.) However,

I do start a few annual herbs from seeds. I find starting most perennial herbs from seeds takes too long, usually at least a year longer than transplants or divisions, and in most cases I can't be sure they will be to my individual taste. When a plant is already growing, I can touch it and smell it to make sure it has a scent to my liking. I start herbs from seeds only if I can't obtain them any other way, such as in the case of some of the unusual varieties of chives, parsley, and cilantro, say, or in the case of herbs that suffer unduly when transplanted, like dill, chervil, and cilantro. When setting out my transplants, if a mat of roots has formed at the bottom of the root ball, I remove it or open it up so the roots won't continue to grow in a tangled mass. I set the plant in the ground at the same height as it was in the container if it's a 4 inches (10 cm) container or smaller, and a little above ground level if it's planted in a one-gallon or larger. I've found the larger root balls settle a little in time and, when planted at ground level, are apt to rot if water puddles in the indentation. I pat the plant in place with gentle hand pressure and water each plant in well to remove air bubbles. If I'm planting on a very hot day or the herb has been in a protected greenhouse, I shade the transplant with a shingle or such, placed on the sunny side of the plant. I then install my ooze irrigation tubing (see "Watering and Irrigation Systems" below for more information) and mulch with a few inches of organic matter. I keep the transplant moist but not soggy for the first few weeks.

STARTING FROM SEEDS

You can grow most herbs from seeds. They can be started indoors in flats or other well-drained containers, outdoors in a cold frame, or, with some easily started annuals, directly in the garden. Starting seeds inside is preferable because it gives your seedlings a warm and safe start. Gardeners in cold or very hot climates are most successful when they start their herb seeds in early spring—the young plant gets well established before summer heat and winter cold. Seedlings are then planted out into the garden after all threat of frost is over. Gardeners in mild climates can transplant seedlings into the garden throughout most of the year. In fact, gardeners in the milder parts of the arid West have great success when they plant just as the rainy season begins.

Propagation from seeds is a complex subject because the cultural needs of seeds vary widely among species. Still, some basic rules apply to most seeding procedures. First, whether starting seeds in the ground or in a container, make sure you have a loose, water-retentive soil that drains well. Good drainage is important because seeds can get waterlogged, and too much water can lead to "damping off," a fungal disease that kills seedlings at the soil line. Commercial starting mixes are usually best since they have been sterilized to remove weed seeds; however, the quality varies greatly from brand to brand, and I find most lack enough nitrogen, so I water with a weak solution of fish emulsion when I plant the seeds, and again a few weeks later.

Smooth the soil surface and plant the seeds at the depth recommended on the package. Pat down the seeds, and water carefully to make the seed bed moist but not soggy. Some seeds need light to germinate; these are best kept moist by laying a sheet of cheesecloth over the seeds and keeping it damp. Remove the cheesecloth as soon as the seeds germinate. When starting seeds outside, protect the seed bed with netting to keep out birds, digging cats, and varmints. If slugs and snails are a problem, circle the area with diatomaceous earth to keep them away, and go out at night with a flashlight to catch any that cross the barrier. If you are starting herbs in containers, put the seedling tray in a warm place to help seeds germinate more quickly.

When starting seeds inside, once seeds have germinated, it's imperative that they immediately be given a quality source of light; otherwise, the new seedlings will be spindly and pale. A greenhouse, sunporch, greenhouse window, or south-facing window with no overhang will suffice, provided it is warm. If one is not available, use grow lights, which are available from home-supply stores or from specialty online vendors. Another option I use if I'm starting seeds and the weather is above 60°F (15.5°C) is to put my seedling trays outside on a table in the sun and protect them with bird netting during the day, bringing them in at night.

Once seedlings are up, keep them moist and, if you have seeded thickly and have crowded plants, thin some out. It's less damaging to do so with small scissors. Cut the little plants out, leaving the remaining seedlings an inch or so

apart. Do not transplant your seedlings until they have their second set of true leaves (the first leaves that sprout from a seed are called seed leaves and usually look different from the later true leaves). If the seedlings are tender, wait until all danger of frost is past before you set them out. In fact, don't put heat-loving basil out until the weather has thoroughly warmed up and is stable. Young plants started indoors or in a greenhouse should be "hardened off" before they are planted in the garden—that is, they should be put outside in a sheltered place for a few days in their containers to let them get used to the differences in temperature, humidity, and air movement outside.

Maintaining the Herb Garden

The backbone of appropriate maintenance is a knowledge of your soil and weather, an ability to recognize basic water- and nutrient-deficiency symptoms, and a familiarity with the plants you grow.

ANNUAL HERBS

Annual herbs are growing machines. As a rule, they need to grow rapidly and with few interruptions so they will produce succulent leaves and have few pest problems. Once the plants are in the ground, continual monitoring for nutrient deficiencies or drought can head off problems. Keep the beds weeded; weeds compete for moisture and nutrients. In normal soil, dill, cilantro, and chervil will not need fertilizer, but basil will probably need a light application of a nitrogen fertilizer such as fish emulsion or fish meal midseason if it is to produce heavily.

PERENNIAL HERBS

As a rule, once perennial herbs are established, they require less routine maintenance than most flowers and vegetables. Fertilizing is not needed for average soil, and pests and diseases are much less a problem than with vegetables and many flowers. There is a short section on pests and diseases in Appendix B; the major tasks needed for herb gardening—annual pruning, weeding, and mulching—are addressed here.

WEEDING

Weeding is needed to make sure unwanted plants don't compete with and overpower your herbs. Be especially vigilant and look for perennial grasses, which if left in place will grow among and over perennial herbs and obliterate them. A good small triangular hoe will help you weed a small area of herbs if you start when the plants are small and easily pulled. If you allow the weeds to get large, then a session of hand pulling will be needed. In all herb plantings, if you apply a good mulch every spring, the need to weed will be minimal after a few years as the herb plants fill in and the annual mulch prevents seeds from sprouting.

PRUNING

Even if you plant your herbs in an informal design, all perennial herbs need occasional pruning. As a rule, a major pruning is needed every spring to force the plants to produce new succulent growth, to keep them from overgrowing an area, and to remove winter damage in cold climates. If you will be harvesting the herbs regularly throughout the growing season, many of the plants will need no further pruning. If you will not be harvesting the herbs in any significant way, and especially in long, mild climates, further pruning midseason after flowering is recommended to prevent the plants from getting woody and sometimes splaying in the middle. I find with herbs growing in my Zone 9 garden that regular light prunings work better than an occasional severe pruning. Basil needs continual harvesting or pruning, or the seed heads develop and the plant yields few leaves for harvesting. Start pruning when the plant is 6 inches (15 cm) tall and keep pinching back new growth and removing the flower spikes. Eventually, though, the plant will probably get ahead of you, so be ready for a major harvest or a pruning with hedge clippers.

MULCHING

Mulching can save the gardener time, effort, and water. A mulch reduces moisture loss, prevents erosion, controls weeds, minimizes soil compaction, and moderates soil temperature. When the mulch is an organic material, it adds nutrients and organic matter to the soil as it decomposes, it helps keep heavy clay porous, sandy soil retain moisture, and it keeps roots cool in summer and from heaving out of the soil in winter. Mulches are often attractive additions to the garden as well. Applying a few inches of organic matter every spring is necessary in most herb gardens to keep them healthy. Mulch with compost from your compost pile, pine needles, composted sawdust, straw, or one of the many agricultural by-products like rice hulls or apple or grape pomace.

COMPOSTING

Compost is the humus-rich result of the decomposition of organic matter, such as leaves and lawn clippings. The objective in maintaining a composting system is to speed up decomposition and centralize the material so you can gather it up and spread it where it will do the most good.

Compost's benefits include providing nutrients to plants in a slow-release, balanced fashion; helping break up clay soils; aiding sandy soils to retain moisture; and correcting pH problems. On top of that, compost is free, it can be made at home, and it is an excellent way to recycle our yard and kitchen "wastes." Compost can be used as a soil additive or a mulch.

There need be no great mystique about composting. To create the environment needed by the decay-causing microorganisms that do all the work, just include the following four ingredients, mixed well: three or four parts "brown" material high in carbon, such as dry leaves, dry grass, or even shredded black-and-white newspaper; one part "green" material high in nitrogen, such as fresh grass clippings, fresh garden trimmings, barnyard manure, or kitchen trimmings such as pea pods and carrot tops; water in moderate amounts, so that the mixture is moist but not soggy; and air to supply oxygen to the microorganisms. Bury the kitchen trimmings within the pile, so as not to attract flies. Cut up large pieces of material. Exclude weeds that have gone to seed, ivy clippings, and Bermuda grass clippings because they can lead to the growth of weeds, ivy, and Bermuda grass in the garden. Do not add meat, fat, diseased plants, woody branches, or cat or dog manure.

I don't stress myself about the proper proportions of compost materials, as long as I have a fairly good mix of materials from the garden. If the decomposition is too slow, it is usually because the pile has too much brown material, is too dry, or needs air. If the pile smells, there is too much green material or it is too wet. To speed up decomposition, I often chop or shred the materials before adding them to the pile, and I may turn the pile occasionally to get additional oxygen to all parts of it. During decomposition, the materials can become quite hot and steamy, which is great; however, it is not mandatory that the compost become extremely hot.

You can make compost in a simple pile, in wire or wood bins, or in rather expensive containers. The size should be about 3 feet x 3 feet x 3 feet (1 m x 1 m x 1 m) for the most efficient decomposition and so that the pile can be easily managed. It can be up to 5 x 5 feet (1.5 x 1.5 m), but it then becomes harder to manage. In a rainy climate it's a good idea to have a cover for the compost. I like to use three bins. I collect the compost materials in one bin, have a working bin, and when that bin is full, I turn the contents into the last bin, where it will finish its decomposition. I sift the finished compost into empty garbage cans so it will not leach its nutrients into the soil. The empty bin is then ready to fill up again. Note: I use compost in the planting hole—I do not use it for mulch.

WATERING AND IRRIGATION SYSTEMS

Even gardeners who live in rainy climates may need to do supplemental watering at specific times during the growing season. For instance, watering is needed for all seed beds and young transplants. One cannot rely upon rain at these times. Therefore, most gardeners need some sort of supplemental watering system and a knowledge of water management.

There is no easy formula for determining the correct amount or frequency of watering. Proper watering takes experience and observation. In addition to the specific watering needs noted above, the water needs of a particular plant depend on soil type, wind conditions, air temperature, and the type of plant. To water properly, you must learn how to recognize water stress symptoms (often a dulling of foliage color as well as the better-known symptoms of drooping leaves and wilting); how much to water (too much is as bad as too little); and how to water. Some general rules are

1. Water deeply. Except for seed beds, most plants need infrequent deep watering rather than frequent light sprinkling.
2. To ensure proper absorption, apply water at a rate slow enough to prevent runoff.
3. Do not use overhead watering systems when the wind is blowing.
4. Try to water early in the morning so that foliage will have time to dry off before nightfall, thus preventing some disease problems. In addition, because of the cooler temperature, less water is lost to evaporation.
5. Test your watering system occasion ally to make sure it is covering the area evenly.
6. Use methods and tools that conserve water. When using a hose, a pistol-grip nozzle will shut off the water while you move from one container or planting bed to another. Soaker hoses, made of either canvas or recycled tires, and other ooze and drip irrigation systems apply water slowly and use water more efficiently than do overhead systems.

Drip, or the related ooze/trickle, irrigation systems are advisable wherever feasible, and most herb gardens are well suited to them. Drip systems deliver water a drop at a time through spaghettilike emitter tubes or plastic pipe with emitters that drip water right onto the root zone of the plant. Because of the time and effort involved in installing one or two emitters per plant, these systems work best for permanent plantings.

Another similar system, called a ooze or porous wall system, delivers water through porous plastic hoses along the whole length of a garden row. After years of experience I find the ooze systems the easiest to install in herb beds if the herb area is level and fairly small. They seem to clog less than emitters and seem to stay in place better. There are different types of ooze systems. Large-diameter tubing, the size of a garden hose, often made from recycled tires, has been available for a number of years; there are also small-diameter, extremely flexible ooze tubing systems. The large ooze tubing is a low-tech, entirely satisfactory system in a few situations. It works well with a large number of perennial herbs planted in a fairly straight line. The large, stiff tubing has little flex, however, and is hard to use in small herb and flower beds because it can't weave itself tightly around numerous small plants. Small-diameter ooze systems can be used in small plantings; while they're fairly expensive, I find them worth the money.

To install these systems requires some thought and time. Look for these systems from either a specialty garden or irrigation source or visit your local plumbing supply store. I find the latter to be the best solution for all my irrigation problems. Over the years I have found that plumbing supply stores offer professional-quality supplies and usually for less money than the so-called inexpensive kits available in home supply stores and some nurseries! In addition to high-quality materials, there are professionals there to help you lay out an irrigation design, so that it is tailored to your garden. Whether you choose an emitter or an ooze system, when you go to buy your tubing, be prepared by bringing a rough drawing of the area to be irrigated—with dimensions, the location of the water source and any slopes, and, if possible, the water pressure at your water source. Let the professionals walk you through the steps and help pick out supplies that would best fit your site.

Problems aside, all forms of drip irrigation are more efficient than furrow or standard overhead watering in delivering water to its precise destination and are well worth considering. They deliver water slowly so it doesn't run off, and they also water deeply, which encourages deep rooting. Drip irrigation also eliminates many herb disease problems, and because so little of the soil surface is moist, there are fewer weeds. Finally, they have the potential to waste a lot less water.

Appendix B:

Disease and Pest Control

The following sections cover a large number of pest and diseases. An individual gardener, however, will encounter few such problems in a lifetime of gardening. Good garden planning, good hygiene, and an awareness of major symptoms will keep problems to a minimum and give you many hours to enjoy your garden and feast on its bounty.

Pest Control

An herb garden is blessed in that it will have far fewer pests than the standard vegetable or rose garden—not only insects but also four-footed pests. Deer and rabbits, say, are seldom interested in most herbs; they prefer to graze on rows of lettuces and beds of succulent perennials instead of small woody plants filled with strong-smelling chemicals. In fact, pest insects as well are seldom drawn to herbs, but in many cases beneficial insects are. Herbs such as cilantro, dill, chervil, thyme, fennel, anise, and caraway all produce many small flowers that provide nectar crucial to many beneficial insects at different stages of their life. Further, many flowering herbs like anise hyssop, chives, mint, oregano, rosemary, sage, borage, chamomile, fennel, lavender, savory, and sweet woodruff not only add color to our gardens but provide nectar and pollen to both domestic and wild bees. When you are aware of the insect world around you, you can be assured that you are helping maintain the balance in your garden, and so benefit not only your herbs but all the plants in your neighborhood.

In a nutshell, few insects are potential garden pests; most are either neutral or beneficial to the garden. Given the chance, the beneficials will do most of your pest control for you, provided that you don't use pesticides, as pesticides are apt to kill the beneficial insects as well as the pests. Like predatory lions stalking zebra, predatory ladybugs (lady beetles) or lacewing larvae will hunt and eat aphids that might be attracted to your chives, say. Or a mini-wasp parasitoid will lay eggs in the aphids. If you spray, even with a so-called benign pesticide such as insecticidal soap or pyrthrum, you'll kill off the lady bugs, lacewings, and that baby parasitoid wasp too. Most insecticides are broad spectrum, which means that they kill insects indiscriminately, not just the pests. In my opinion, organic gardeners who regularly use organic broad-spectrum insecticides have missed this point. If you use an "organic" pesticide, you may actually be eliminating a truly organic means of pest control, the beneficial insects.

Unfortunately, many gardeners are not aware of the benefits of the predator-prey relationship and are not able to recognize beneficial insects. The following sections will help you identify both helpful and pest organisms. A more detailed aid for identifying insects is Rodale's *Color Handbook of Garden Insects*, by Anna Carr. A hand lens is an invaluable and inexpensive tool that will also help you identify the insects in your garden.

PREDATORS AND PARASITOIDS

Insects that feed on other insects are divided into two types, the predators and the parasitoids. Predators are mobile. They stalk plants looking for such plant feeders as aphids and mites. Parasitoids, on the other hand, are insects that develop in or on the bodies, pupae, or eggs of other host insects. Most parasitoids are minute wasps or flies whose larvae (young stages) eat other insects from within. Some of these wasps are small enough to live within an aphid or an insect egg. Or one parasitoid egg can divide into thousands of identical cells, which in turn develop into thousands of identical miniwasps, which can then consume an entire caterpillar. Though nearly invisible to most gardeners, parasitoids are the most specific and effective means of insect control.

The predator-prey relationship can be a fairly stable situation; when the natural system is working properly, pest insects inhabiting the garden along with the predators and parasites seldom become a problem. Sometimes, though, the system breaks down. For example, a number of imported pests have taken hold in this country. Unfortunately, when such organisms were brought here, their natural predators did not accompany them. Two notorious examples are a problem with some herbs: the European brown snail and the Japanese beetle. Neither organism has natural enemies in this country that provide sufficient controls. Where such organisms occur, it is sometimes necessary to use physical means or selective pesticides that kill only the problem insect. Weather extremes sometime produce an imbalance as well. For example, long

stretches of hot, dry weather favor grasshoppers that sometimes eat basil or other lush herbs, because the diseases that keep these insects in check are more prevalent under moist conditions. There are other situations in which the predator-prey relationship gets out of balance because many gardening practices inadvertently work in favor of the pests. For example, when gardeners spray with broad-spectrum pesticides regularly, not all the insects in the garden are killed-and since predators and parasitoids generally reproduce much more slowly than do the pests, regular spraying usually tips the balance in favor of the pests. Further, all too often the average yard has few plants that produce nectar for beneficial insects; instead it is filled with grass and shrubs, so that when a few plants of chives or a row of basil are put in, the new plants attract the aphids, but there are no nectar plants to attract the beneficials. Not only will these practices help you create an herb garden free of most pest problems, but the herbs themselves can probably help eliminate other pest problems you or your neighbors have struggled with for years.

ATTRACTING BENEFICIAL INSECTS

Besides reducing your use of pesticides, the key to keeping a healthy balance in your garden is providing a diversity of plants, including plenty of nectar- and pollen-producing plants. Nectar is the primary food of the adult stage, and some larval stages, of many beneficial insects. Many herbs are among the plants that attract beneficial insects. And the very small flowers on parsley, cilantro, and dill are just what many of the tiny beneficial insects need.

Following are a few of the predatory and parasitoid insects that are helpful in the garden. Their preserva-

tion and protection should be a major goal of your pest-control strategy.

Ground Beetles and their larvae are all predators. Most adult ground beetles are fairly large black beetles that scurry out from under your lavender or savory plants when you uncover them. Their favorite foods are soft-bodied larvae like root maggots, some even eat snails and slugs. If supplied with an undisturbed place to live, like your compost area or groupings of perennial plantings including herbs, ground beetles will be long-lived residents of your garden.

Lacewings are one of the most effective insect predators in the home garden. They are small green or brown gossamer-winged insects that in their adult stage eat flower nectar, pollen, aphid honeydew, and sometimes aphids and mealy-bugs. In the larval stage they look like little tan alligators. Called aphid lions, the larvae are fierce predators of aphids, mealybugs, mites, thrips, and whiteflies—all occasional pests of herbs.

Lady Beetles (Ladybugs) are the best known of the beneficial garden insects. Actually, there are about four hundred species of lady beetles in North America alone. They come in a variety of colors and markings in addition to the familiar red with black spots, but they are never green. Lady beetles and their fierce-looking alligator-shaped larvae eat aphids, mealybugs, and other small insects.

Spiders are close relatives of insects. There are hundreds of species, and they are some of the most effective controllers of pest insects.

Syrphid flies (also called flower flies or hover flies) look like small bees hovering over flowers, but they have only two wings. Most have yellow and black stripes on their body. Their larvae are small green maggots that reside on leaves, eating aphids, mealybugs, other small insects, and mites.

Wasps are a large family of insects with transparent wings. Unfortunately, the few that sting have given wasps a bad name. In fact, all wasps are either insect predators or parasitoids. The parasitoid adult female lays her eggs in such insects as aphids and caterpillars, and the developing larvae devour the host.

PESTS

The following pests are sometimes a problem in the herb garden.

Aphids are soft-bodied, small, green, black, pink, gold, or gray insects that can produce many generations in one season. They suck plant juices and exude honeydew. Sometimes leaves under the aphids turn black from a secondary mold growing on the nutrient-rich honeydew. Aphids are primarily a problem on parsley, chives, chervil, and sometimes basil. A buildup of aphids can indicate that the plant is under stress—is the basil getting enough water, or sunlight, say? Check first to see if stress is a problem and then try to correct it. If there is a large infestation, look for aphid mummies and other natural enemies mentioned above. Mummies are swollen brown or metallic-looking aphids. Inside the mummy a wasp parasitoid is growing. They are valuable, so keep them. To remove aphids generally, wash the foliage with a strong blast of water and cut back the foliage if they persist. Fertilize and water the plant, and check on it in a few days. Repeat with the water spray a few more times. In extreme situations spray with insecticidal soap or a neem product.

While many **beetles** are beneficial insects, a number are garden pests, including cucumber and Japanese beetles. Cucumber beetles are ladybug-like green or yellow-green beetles with either black stripes or black spots. Japanese beetles are fairly large and metallic blue or green with coppery wings. Both sometimes eat holes in sorrel, basil, and other succulent herbs.

Beetles such as Japanese and cucumber beetles, if not in great numbers, can be controlled by hand picking-in the morning is best, when the beetles are slower. Toss them or knock them into a bowl or bucket of soapy water. Larger populations may need more control, however. Try a spray of insecticidal soap first; if you're not successful, use neem or pyrethrum. Japanese beetles were accidentally introduced into the United States early in this century and are now a serious problem in the eastern part of the country. The larval stage (a grub) lives on the roots of grasses, and the adult beetle skeletonizes the leaves of many plants and chews on flowers and buds. Certain species of beneficial nematodes have proved effective in controlling the larvae of Japanese beetles. Milky-spore, a naturally occurring soil-borne disease, is also used to control the beetles in the larval stage, although the disease is slow to work.

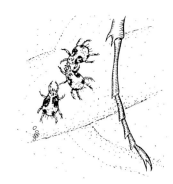

Mites are among the few arachnids (spiders and their kin) that pose a problem in the garden. Mites are so small that a hand lens is usually needed to see them. They become a problem when they reproduce in great numbers and suck on the leaves of such herbs as angelica, lavender, lemon verbena, mints, oregano, rosemary, sage, savory, and thyme, especially when these plants are grown in the house. A symptom of serious mite damage is stippling on the leaves in the form of tiny white or yellow spots, sometimes accompanied by tiny webs. The major natural predators of mites are predatory mites. Mite-eating thrips and syrphid flies also help in mite control.

Mites are most likely to thrive on dusty leaves and in dry, warm weather. A routine foliage wash and misting of sensitive plants helps control mites. Mites are seldom a serious problem unless you have used heavy-duty pesticides that kill off predatory mites or you are growing plants in the house. Cut back plants and if you're using heavy-duty pesticides, stop the applications, and the balance could return. Serious infestations usually are controlled by using horticultural oil. For plants in the house, cut back foliage, wash it well, quarantine the plants, and apply refined horticultural oil. If mites persist, discard the plants. Caution: Always tend to plants with mites last, or wash tools well, as mites like to hitchhike on tools to other plants.

Nematodes are microscopic round worms that inhabit the soil in most of the United States, particularly in the Southeast. Most nematode species live on decaying matter or are predatory on other nematodes, insects, algae, or bacteria. (See "Beneficial Nematodes" below.) A few types are parasitic, attaching themselves to the roots of some of our most popular perennial herbs, including lavender and rosemary. The symptoms of nematode damage are stunned-looking plants and small swellings or lesions on the roots.

To control nematodes, keep your soil high in organic matter (to encourage fungi and predatory nematodes, both of which act as biological controls). Some success has been recorded by using applications of beneficial nematodes available from insectaries. If all else fails, grow your herbs in containers with sterilized soil.

Snails and slugs are not insects, of course, but mollusks. They avoid most herbs but relish the leafy, succulent sorrel and basils. They feed at night and can go dormant for months in times of drought or low food supply.

In the absence of effective natural enemies (a few snail eggs are consumed by predatory beetles and ear-

wigs), several snail-control strategies can be recommended. Since snails and slugs are most active after rain or irrigation, go out and destroy them on such nights. Only repeated forays will provide adequate control. Planter boxes with a strip of copper applied along the top perimeter boards keep slugs and snails out-they wont cross the barrier. Any overhanging leaves that can provide a bridge into the bed will defeat the barrier. You will get some control by putting out shallow containers filled with cheap beer to within an inch of the top. The pests crawl in and are not able to crawl out.

Whiteflies are sometimes a problem in mild-winter areas of the country, as well as in greenhouses nationwide and on sages, mints, lemon verbena, and rosemary. Whiteflies are a persistent problem on some plants, particularly if they are planted up against a building or fence where air circulation is limited. Move plants out into the open if possible and see if the problem disappears. In the garden, birds, Encarsia wasps and other parasitoids usually provide adequate whitefly control.

Occasionally, especially in cool weather or in greenhouses, whitefly populations may begin to cause serious plant damage (wilting and slowing of growth or flowering). Look under the leaves to determine whether the scalelike, immobile larvae and pupae are present in large numbers. If so, wash them off with water from your hose. Repeat the washing three days in a row. Adults can be trapped by the following method: Apply Stickum or Tanglefoot to a yellow file folder. Hold the folder open near the affected plant and give the plant a shake. The adult whiteflies will fly to the yellow folder and adhere to the sticky surface. Or try vacuuming up the adults with a handheld vacuum early in the day while the weather

is still cool and they are less active. Insecticidal soap sprays or a refined horticultural oil can be quite effective as well.

PEST CONTROLS
Beneficial Nematodes (Entomopathogenic Nematodes) are microscopic round worms. Many nematodes are selective predators of certain insects, especially soil-dwelling insects. They can be purchased to control various pests, including Japanese beetle and cucumber beetle larvae. Most beneficial nematodes must be applied mixed with water and need warm weather to survive. Be sure you are using the species for the pest you have and read the directions carefully for application. Since they are selective, they do not harm earthworms or other organisms.

Insecticidal Soap Sprays are effective against many pest insects, including caterpillars, aphids, mites, and whiteflies. They can be purchased, or you can make a soap spray at home. I recommend purchasing insecticidal soap, such as the one made by Safer Corporation, as it has been carefully formulated to give the most effective control with the least risk to your plants. If you do make your own, use a liquid dishwashing soap; do not use caustic or dermacial soaps.

Horticultural oils have been used for many years as dormant sprays on fruit trees. Today most horticultural oils are lightweight "summer" or "superior" horticultural oils that have been refined to remove the compounds that damage the leaves of growing plants. The more refined oil can be used on some herbs to control pest insects and diseases; however, they do smother beneficial insects as well as the pests. Follow the directions for summer concentrations. Always test the oil on a small part of the plant first, as some plants are very sensitive to oil sprays and will burn or lose their leaves. In addition, don't use horticultural oil on very hot days or on plants that are moisture-stressed.

Neem-oil extracts, which are derived from the neem tree (*Azadirachta indica*), have relatively low toxicity to mammals but are effective insecticides against a wide range of insects, including different types of aphids, cucumber beetles, and spider mites. They work in a variety of different ways. Neem is still fairly new in the United States. Although neem was thought at first to be harmless to beneficial insects, studies now show that some parasitoid beneficial insects that feed on neem-treated pest insects were unable to survive to adulthood.

Pyrethrum, a botanical insecticide, is toxic to a wide range of insects but has relatively low toxicity to most mammals and breaks down quickly in the presence of sunlight. The active ingredients in pyrethrum are pyrethins derived from chrysanthemum flowers. Do not confuse pyrethrum with pyrethoids, which are much more toxic synthetics that do not biodegrade nearly as quickly as pyrethrum. Many pyrethrums have a synergist, piperonyl butoxide (PBO) added to increase the effectiveness. However, there is evidence that PRO may affect the human nervous system. Try to use pyrethrums without PBO added. Wear gloves, goggles, and a respirator when using pyrethrum.

Diseases

Plant diseases are potentially far more damaging to your herbs than are most insects. Diseases are also more difficult to control because they usually grow inside the plant, and plants do not respond with immune mechanisms comparable to those that protect animals. Consequently, most plant disease control strategies feature prevention rather than control. Hence, the constant admonition to plant most herbs in soil with good drainage.

Cultural Techniques To keep diseases under control it is very important to plant the "right plant in the right place." For instance, many herbs, such as lavender or sage, prefer a dry environment and will often develop root rot in soil that is continually wet. Check the cultural needs of a plant before placing it in your garden. Proper light, exposure, temperature, fertilization, and moisture are important factors in disease control. Diseased plants should always be discarded, not composted. The entries for individual plants in the *Encyclopedia of Culinary Herbs* give specific cultural information.

The most common diseases of herbs are described below.

Damping Off is caused by a parasitic fungus that lives near the soil surface and attacks new plants in their early seedling stage. It causes them to wilt and fall over just where they emerge from the soil. This fungus thrives under dark, humid conditions, so it can often be thwarted by keeping the seedlings in a bright, well-ventilated place in fast-draining soil.

Powdery mildew is an occasional problem on a few herbs and is most apt to strike in summer and fall. This fungus disease manifests as a powdery white growth on the leaves. Herbs occasionally susceptible to it are cilantro, lemon balm, and tarragon. Make sure the plant has good air circulation and is otherwise healthy. Spraying with refined horticultural oil or lime sulfur will help control mildew.

A number of fungi cause **root rot**. The classic symptom of root rot is wilting—even after a rain or when a plant is well watered. Sometimes the wilting starts with only a few branches, other times the whole plant wilts. Plants are often stunted and yellow as well. The diagnosis is complete when the dead plant is pulled up to reveal rotten, black roots. Root rot is a common problem with many perennial herbs, and it is most often caused by poor drainage. There is no cure for root rot once it involves the whole plant. Remove and destroy the plant and correct the drainage problem.

Resources

The following is a sampling of the many online vendors of plants, seeds, and gardening and cooking supplies. Many of these sites offer useful information on growing, maintaining, preserving and cooking with herbs.

SEED, PLANT AND GARDENING SUPPLIERS

Chiltern Seeds (UK)
www.chilternseeds.co.uk
Large variety of seeds, including herbs and edible flowers

Artistic Gardens/Le Jardin du Gourmet
www.artisticgardens.com
Herb plants and seeds

Bonnie Plants
www.bonnieplants.com
Herbs and vegetable seeds (no online purchase. Retailers can be found via website). Site includes tips and recipes.

Chef's Catalog
www.chefs-garden.com
Herbs, vegetables, edible flowers

Fox Hollow Herb Farm
www.foxhollowherbs.com
Herbs, vegetables, flowers, heirlooms

Gardener's Supply Company
www.gardeners.com
Gardening tools and supplies

Great Lakes Hops
www.greatlakeshops.com
Prime source of hops

The Gourmet Gardeners
www.thegourmetgardeners.org
Herbs, vegetables, edible flowers, seeds

Grow Organic
www.groworganic.com
Herbs, fruits, vegetables, gardening supplies

The Growers Exchange
www.thegrowers-exchange.com
Culinary, Native American, rare/ unusual herbs and medicinal herbs

The Herb Exchange
theherbexchange.com
Herb plants and seeds, information

Johnny's Selected Seeds
www.johnnyseeds.com
Excellent selection of herb and vegetable seeds; unusual and European varieties; farm seed, cover crops, tools and supplies

Logee's Greenhouses
www.logees.com
Herb pants and seeds, ornamental perennial plants, many unusual and tender varieties

The Natural Gardening Company
www.naturalgardening.com
Vegetable, herbs, flowers, and a good range of supplies and accessories

Nichols Garden Nursery
www.nicholsgardennursery.com
Wide selection of interesting European salad greens, herbs, and other vegetable

Park Seed
www.parkseed.com
Herbs, flowers, fruits, vegetables

Organically Grown
www.organicallygrown.com
Good selection of European varieties of vegetables and herbs

Raintree Nursery
www.raintree nursery.com
A source of hops

Redwood City Seed Company
www.ecoseeds.com
Specializes in endangered cultivated plants. Download catalog online, order by phone

Renee's Garden
www.reneesgarden.com
Organic, non-GMO seeds, Carefully selected European specialties

Richter's Herbs (CA)
www.richters.com
Extensive selection of herbs seeds and plants, unusual gourmet vegetables and European varieties

Seeds Savers Exchange
www.seedsavers.org
Seed-sharing/swapping community for vegetables, fruits, herbs and information

Seeds of Change
www.seedsofchange.com
Vegetables, herbs, prepared rice dishes

The Thyme Garden Herb Co.
www.thymegarden.com
Source of herb and hop plants

Well-Sweep Herb Farm
wellsweep.com
Extensive catalog of common and uncommon seeds, plants and dried herbs. No shipment of live plants to AZ, CA, OR or WA

COOKING SUPPLIERS

Balduccis
www.balduccis.com
Food products, fancy herbs and seasonings

Chef's Catalog
www.chefscatalog.com
Professional and home cooking supplies

Dean and DeLuca
www.deandeluca.com
Food products, fancy herbs and oils, cooking equipment

Penzeys
www.penzeys.com
Specializes in herbs and spices

Sur La Table
www.surlatable.com
Cooking equipment

Williams-Sonoma
www.williams-sonoma.com
Cooking equipment

Books and Other References

Alley, Lynn. *Cooking with Herbs: 50 Simple Recipes for Fresh Flavor.* Kansas City: Andrews McMeel Publishing LLC, 2013.

Belsinger, Susan and Arthur O. Tucker. *The Culinary Herbal: Growing and Preserving 97 Flavorful Herbs.* Portland, OR: Timber Press, 2016.

Creasy, Rosalind. *Edible Landscaping, 2nd Ed.* Berkeley: Counterpoint Ress, 2010.

De La Foret, Rosalee. *Alchemy of Herbs: Transform Everyday Ingredients into Foods and Remedies That Heal.* Carlsbad, CA: Hay House Inc., 2017.

DK. *The Cook's Herb Garden.* New York: DK, 2010.

The editors of Sunset magazines and Sunset books. *Sunset National Garden Book.* Menlo Park, CA: Sunset Publishing Co., 1997.

_____ *Sunset Western Garden Book.* Menlo Park, CA.: Sunset Publishing Co., 1995.

Fewell, Amy K. and Joel Salatin. *The Homesteader's Herbal Companion: The Ultimate Guide to Growing, Preserving, and Using Herbs.* Lanham, MD: Lyons Press, 2018.

Fisher, Joe and Dennis Fisher. *The Homebrewer's Garden, 2nd Ed.: How to Grow, Prepare & Use Your Own Hops, Malts & Brewing Herbs.* North Adams, MA: Storey Publishing, 2016.

Hartung, Tammi. *Homegrown Herbs: A Complete Guide to Growing, Using, and Enjoying More than 100 Herbs.* North Adams, MA: Storey Publishing, 2011.

Gilbertie, Sal and Larry Sheehan. *Herb Gardening from the Ground Up: Everything You Need to Know about Growing Your Favorite Herbs.* Berkeley: Ten Speed Press, 2012.

Hopkinson, Patricia, Diane Miske, Jerry Parsons, and Holly Shimizu. *Herb Gardening (American Garden Guides).* New York: Pantheon Books, 1994.

Kowalchik, Claire, Wllliam H. Hy|ton, ed. and Anna Car, ed. *Rodale's Illustrated Encyclopedia of Herbs.* Emmaus, Pa.: Rodale Press, 1998.

Lathrop, Norma Jean. *Herbs: How to Select, Grow and Enjoy.* Tucson: H. P. Books, 1981.

McBride, Kami. *The Herbal Kitchen: Bring Lasting Health to You and Your Family with 50 Easy-to-Find Common Herbs and Over 250 Recipes, 2nd. Ed.* Newburyport, MA: Conari Press, 2019.

McGee, Rose Marie Nichols and Maggie Stuckey *McGee and Stuckey's Bountiful Container: Create Container Gardens of Vegetables, Herbs, Fruits and Edible Flowers.* New York: Workman Publishing Co. Inc., 2002.

Norman, Jill. *Herbs & Spices: the Cook's Reference.* New York: DK, 2015.

Olkowski, William, Sheila Daar, and Helga Olkowski. *The Gardener's Guide to Common Sense Pest Control, Rev. Ed.* Newtown, CT: Taunton Press, 2013.

Saville, Carole. *Exotic Herbs.* New York: Henry Holt and Co., 1997.

Shepherd, Renee. *More Recipes from a Kitchen Garden.* Felton, CA. Shepherd, Renee, Shepherd's Garden Publishing, 2003.

Shepherd, Renee. *Recipes from a Kitchen Garden.* Felton, CA.: Shepherds Garden Publishing, 1987.

Shepherd, Renee. *The Renee's Garden Cookbook.* Felton, CA. Shepherd, Renee, Shepherd's Garden Publishing, 2014.

Smith, Miranda. *Your Backyard Herb Garden: A Gardener's Guide to Growing, Using and Enjoying Herbs Organically.* Emmaus, PA: Rodale Press, 1997.

Wilson, Jim. *Landscaping With Herbs.* Boston: Houghton Mifflin 1994.

MAGAZINES:

The Essential Herbal
essentialherbal.com

The Herb Quarterly
www.herbquarterly.com

Mother Earth News
www.motherearthnews.com

WEBSITES:

American Horticulture Society.
www.ahsgardening.org/gardening-resources
Source of heat zone and hardiness maps, publications, gardening information

Acknowledgments

My garden is the foundation for my books, photography, and recipes. For nearly twelve months of the year we toil to keep it beautiful and bountiful. Unlike most gardens, as it is a photo studio and trial plot, it must look glorious, be healthy, and produce for the kitchen. To complicate the maintenance, all the beds are changed at least twice a year. Needless to say it is a large undertaking. For two decades a quartet of talented organic gardener/cooks have not only given it hundreds of hours of loving attention, but they have also been generous with their vast knowledge of plants. Together we have forged our concept of gardening and cooking, much of which I share with you in this series of garden cookbooks. I wish to thank Wendy Krupnick for giving the garden such a strong foundation and Joe Queirolo for maintaining it for many years and lending it such a gentle and sure hand. For the last decade Jody Main and Duncan Minalga have helped me expand my garden horizons. No matter how complex the project they enthusiastically rise to the occasion.

In the kitchen, I am most fortunate to have Gudi Riter, a very talented cook who developed many of her skills in Germany and France. I thank her for the help she provides as we create recipes and present them in all their glory. I want to thank Carole Saville who has generously shared her vast knowledge of herbs and given me a firm footing. Over the years we have collaborated on magazine columns and books, and much of her talent appears in these pages. Herbs have different requirements, depending on the climate in which they are grown. I dep end on herb mavens; Rose Marie Nichols McGee of Nichols Garden Nursery in Oregon, Jim Wilson in South Carolina, Madeline Hill and Gwen Barkley in Texas, Louise Hyde at Well-Sweep Herb Farm in New Jersey, Lucinda Hutson in Texas, and Ron Zimmerman in Washington for their expertise, and I thank them for sharing their gardens. I thank Dayna Lane for her steady hand and editorial assistance. In addi-

tion to day-to-day compilations, she joins me on our constant search for the most effective organic pest controls, superior herb varieties, and the best sources for plants. I would also like to thank a large supporting cast: my late husband Robert for many years of quality technical advice and loving support; my daughter-in-law Julie Creasy who is always available for recipe testing or a photo shoot; Nancy Favier for her occasional help in the garden and office; Jesse Ziff Cool, owner of Flea Street Cafe in California, for her wonderful recipes; Renee Shepherd of Renees Garden, and Cathy Barash, editor of Meredith Books, for sharing her information and enthusiasm; Jane Whitfield, Linda Gunnarson, and David Humphrey, who were integral to the initial vision of this book and Marcie Hawthorne for the lovely drawings. Finally, heartfelt thanks to publisher Eric Oey and the team at Tuttle—Terri Jadick, June Chong and Irene Ho—for bringing this edition to life.

Published by Tuttle Publishing, an imprint of
Periplus Editions (HK) Ltd.

www.tuttlepublishing.com

ISBN 978-0-8048-5230-2
*(previously published as The Edible Herb Garden
ISBN 978-962-593-291-0)*

LCCN 2019461166

Revised Edition
26 25 24 23
10 9 8 7 6 5 4 3 2

Printed in China   2312EP

DISTRIBUTED BY

North America, Latin America & Europe
Tuttle Publishing
364 Innovation Drive
North Clarendon, VT 05759-9436 U.S.A.
Tel: 1 (802) 773-8930
Fax: 1 (802) 773-6993
info@tuttlepublishing.com
www.tuttlepublishing.com

Asia Pacific
Berkeley Books Pte. Ltd.
3 Kallang Sector #04-01
Singapore 349278
Tel: (65) 6741 2178
Fax: (65) 6741 2179
inquiries@periplus.com.sg
www.tuttlepublishing.com

TUTTLE PUBLISHING® is a registered trademark of
Tuttle Publishing, a division of Periplus Editions (HK) Ltd.

"Books to Span the East and West"

Tuttle Publishing was founded in 1832 in the small New England town of Rutland, Vermont [USA]. Our core values remain as strong today as they were then—to publish best-in-class books which bring people together one page at a time. In 1948, we established a publishing outpost in Japan—and Tuttle is now a leader in publishing English-language books about the arts, languages and cultures of Asia. The world has become a much smaller place today and Asia's economic and cultural influence has grown. Yet the need for meaningful dialogue and information about this diverse region has never been greater. Over the past seven decades, Tuttle has published thousands of books on subjects ranging from martial arts and paper crafts to language learning and literature—and our talented authors, illustrators, designers and photographers have won many prestigious awards. We welcome you to explore the wealth of information available on Asia at **www.tuttlepublishing.com**.